W9-AUK-023

Think Your

Troubles Away

TARCHER/PENGUIN TITLES
BY ERNEST HOLMES

365 Science of Mind
A New Design for Living
The Art of Life
Creative Mind
Creative Mind and Success
Discover a Richer Life
The Essential Ernest Holmes
The Hidden Power of the Bible
Living Without Fear
Love and Law: The Unpublished Teachings
Prayer
The Science of Mind: The Definitive Edition
This Thing Called You
The Science of Mind: The Complete Edition
It's Up to You
Think Your Troubles Away

JEREMY P. TARCHER/PENGUIN

a member of Penguin Group (USA) Inc.

New York

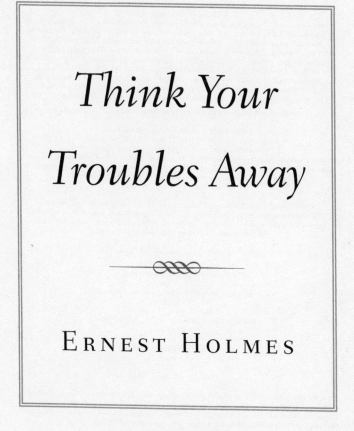

Think Your Troubles Away

ERNEST HOLMES

Compiled and edited by
WILLIS KINNEAR

JEREMY P. TARCHER/PENGUIN
Published by the Penguin Group
Penguin Group (USA) Inc., 375 Hudson Street, New York, New York 10014, USA · Penguin Group
(Canada), 90 Eglinton Avenue East, Suite 700, Toronto, Ontario M4P 2Y3, Canada (a division of
Pearson Penguin Canada Inc.) · Penguin Books Ltd, 80 Strand, London WC2R 0RL, England ·
Penguin Ireland, 25 St Stephen's Green, Dublin 2, Ireland (a division of Penguin Books Ltd) ·
Penguin Group (Australia), 250 Camberwell Road, Camberwell, Victoria 3124, Australia (a division
of Pearson Australia Group Pty Ltd) · Penguin Books India Pvt Ltd, 11 Community Centre,
Panchsheel Park, New Delhi–110 017, India · Penguin Group (NZ), 67 Apollo Drive, Rosedale,
North Shore 0632, New Zealand (a division of Pearson New Zealand Ltd) · Penguin Books
(South Africa) (Pty) Ltd, 24 Sturdee Avenue, Rosebank, Johannesburg 2196, South Africa

Penguin Books Ltd, Registered Offices: 80 Strand, London WC2R 0RL, England

First Jeremy P. Tarcher/Penguin edition 2010
Copyright © 2010 by the United Church of Religious Science
Originally published in 1963 by Science of Mind Publications
All rights reserved. No part of this book may be reproduced, scanned, or distributed in any printed or
electronic form without permission. Please do not participate in or encourage piracy of copyrighted
materials in violation of the author's rights. Purchase only authorized editions.
Published simultaneously in Canada
Most Tarcher/Penguin books are available at special quantity discounts for bulk purchase
for sales promotions, premiums, fund-raising, and educational needs. Special books or book
excerpts also can be created to fit specific needs. For details, write Penguin Group (USA) Inc.
Special Markets, 375 Hudson Street, New York, NY 10014.

Library of Congress Cataloging-in-Publication Data

Holmes, Ernest, 1887–1960.
Think your troubles away / Ernest Holmes.
p.   cm.
"Originally published in 1963 by Science of Mind Publications."
ISBN 978-1-58542-841-0
1. New Thought.   I. Title.
BF639.H6356   2010   2010037340
299'.93—dc22

Printed in the United States of America
1   3   5   7   9   10   8   6   4   2

BOOK DESIGN BY NICOLE LAROCHE
While the author has made every effort to provide accurate telephone numbers and Internet addresses
at the time of publication, neither the publisher nor the author assumes any responsibility for errors, or
for changes that occur after publication. Further, the publisher does not have any control over and does
not assume any responsibility for author or third-party websites or their content.

Contents

PART THREE

Thoughts Become Things

Foreword

This Annual Edition of *Science of Mind* magazine is the third of these publications to bring together the miscellaneous writings of Ernest Holmes.

Once again the source of this material has been the early issues of *Science of Mind* magazine which started publication in 1927. For many years Dr. Holmes's writings which appeared in these issues have been unavailable to the general public. It is felt that they possess such a dynamic quality and spiritual insight that they should be brought to light, becoming a permanent and valuable contribution to the literature dealing with the Science of Mind.

Ernest Holmes was one of the great religious philosophers of our day, and his universal approach to the basic and innate spiritual yearnings of all men won him fame and worldwide recognition. His formulation of the teaching of the Science of Mind cuts across all religious barriers and greatly influences the lives of all who come to know it.

His fundamental philosophy is extremely simple, yet it has had a profound and tremendous impact on the thinking of countless people in all walks of life. He claimed no originality for his ideas, but said that they were a synthesis of the best yet learned in man's three great fields of inquiry: science, philosophy, and religion.

Many others have incorporated his ideas into their own way of thinking and teaching, but here we find in all their purity many of the basic concepts which have changed and will continue to change the lives of all those who discover them and use them.

WILLIS KINNEAR

I AM WHAT I KNOW
THOUGHTS ARE THINGS

Introduction

You are what you know, and the corollary of that is this: What you now know about yourself is also what you will become.

This idea may be more simply stated by the familiar expression "Thoughts are things," and there is more truth in this statement than you may realize.

You know that a thought always precedes an act on your part. Also you know that an idea is first formed in one's mind before some tangible manifestation appears, such as the making of a chair, the building of a bridge, the creation of a big corporation, or even the baking of a cake. Obvious illustrations to say the least. But, on the other hand, perhaps there is

much more involved, much more resulting from your thoughts
and your patterns of thinking than you are aware of.

Happiness stems from a way of thinking and not from
any external factor. Your emotions and their resultant effects
are not controlled by outward conditions, but by your inner
direction of them. As much as you would like to believe that
your state of health is determined by things outside yourself, you have now been told by leading authorities that even
100% of your physical ailments, in many respects, have their
origin in the way you think.

It might be said that each thought you have, good or bad,
is a seed that is planted in fertile soil and grows and produces
fruit according to the basic idea imbedded in it. Regardless
of the nature of your present experience in daily living, in
some way or other you can trace that experience back to a
thought-seed that you have planted and nourished within
your own consciousness!

Yes, thoughts are things. So, if you find that your life
is not all that you would have it be, it becomes necessary to
change your patterns of thinking. You need to uproot those
undesirable thoughts you have planted and replace them
with others more to your liking.

This may sound simple, and it is. But in order to do this
there needs to be an understanding of who you are, what you
are, and the nature of the universe in which you live. The

UPROOT NEG THOUGHTS

world in which you live does operate in a harmonious and lawful manner. And it is only by understanding the laws of life that you may be able to cooperate with them and use them to your advantage rather than disadvantage.

To make full and constructive use of the axiom "Thoughts are things" requires that you come to realize that there is a Power in the universe greater than you are, and that you can use It. This Power can and does always respond to you, but only in the manner in which you actually use It, not in the manner you would just like to have It respond.

The material in this volume can show you the way to so relate yourself to the great spiritual Power in the universe that you may come to think in a creative and constructive manner so that the things in your life are outward manifestations of your inner thoughts which you have learned to properly control and direct.

In this way you can come to experience more of the peace, perfection, good, beauty, power, and joy which reside at the center of that Divine creative Source of all things.

You have problems just like everyone else, but the solving of these troubles is a matter of the way you think. Wrong thinking created them; right thinking can resolve them and cause them to fade away.

W.K.

Think Your

Troubles Away

PART ONE

New Foundations for Thinking

For the most part you seem to be living in an age of turmoil. Both the external world and your inner world of the mind appear to be in a state of confusion. There seems to be a lack of stability, of what to think and what should be a proper reaction to things and events. But then most people have felt that way about the period in which they have lived.

However, throughout the ages there have been those who have found enjoyment, peace, and contentment in spite of the condition of the world around them.

What they have been able to discover you can discover. But the secret, if there is any, lies in the fundamental basic mental attitude you are able to establish. Your mind, needs a firm, intelligent, and emotionally satisfying concept of the nature of Life, and a recognition of your position in It and relationship to It.

It is your basic concepts in this respect that color all of your *thinking, that determine the nature of your thoughts which become the things in your life, and enable you to adequately deal with all your problems.*

In the ideas advanced in the following pages you can find a surety and a security on which you can build a better life.

I.

A New Idea

That we are entering a new cycle of experience is certain. It is impossible to pick up any periodical of the day without noting some evidence of the change of thought that is going on. We hear of the new psychology, the new science, the new religion, the new universe. What does this mean? and where is it leading us?

Has the faith of our forefathers been shattered on the rocks of a cold science? Has the shock which religion has suffered in recent years undermined our spiritual forces? Has our new philosophy solved the riddle of the universe? Are we lost in the fog of speculative theories? Is anything left that is certain? What can we believe? On all sides these questions are being asked, and whoever finds a reasonable answer will have the world for an audience.

There is no lack of interest. Life, hope, and love are still the dominant factors in people's thoughts. God may be a myth, but people still long for Divine guidance. Immortality may be an illusion, but people still hope that the future will not be an oblivion. Religion may be a mental hallucination, but people still have a mystic sense of Reality, an intuitive perception of Something higher. Aspiration may have turned into the ashes of dead hopes, but the urge to go on still pushes us forward. Science may have failed to find the ultimate Cause, but people still sense an invisible Presence. The age-old question, unanswered, still stimulates the interest: From whence the spirit—whither bound the soul? It is impossible to avoid the issue.

We are so constituted that we must go on. We cannot stop. People have always believed in some kind of God and in some type of savior. They still believe. The will to believe is our strongest passion, our greatest incentive, our constant source of inspiration.

Can we by searching find God? We have looked everywhere. The search has been intense, exhilarating, persistent. But have we found Him? Some will answer *yes*, and others *no*. Those who answer *yes* have the right to be heard as well as those who answer *no*. Both are sincere and each is motivated by the same purpose—necessity.

Anyone who doubts that the quest of man is after God is unacquainted with the human mind. The two great desires of man are for unity with the Spirit and for the realization of immortality. Beside these all other desires sink into utter insignificance. To question this is to admit a profound ignorance of the workings of people's thought.

Can such a universal demand be without a foundation in Reality? And if we have failed to find God or failed to realize the eternity of our own being, may it not be because we have failed to realize what God and existence mean?

God is not a person, yet God is more than a principle. The creative insistence of the universe, the emotional background of all incentive is God—the Urge and the act, the Thinker and that which is thought, the Conceiver and the conceived. Cause and effect are but two sides of the same coin. Who looks for God as a person must look into the personification. The Universe may be impersonal as law and as essence, but It is forever personifying Itself. It is revealed in creation.

Only the one who loves comprehends the meaning and the depth of love. Love declares itself through its personification. It is known by its works. It is as real as we make it. It is not a platitude, but a Divine passion. If we would know God as love we must become love. Those who have done this claim to know God as love. Dare we deny the validity of this claim? Can the coldly skeptical sense the Divine emotion of a love which proceeds from the fundamental unity and includes the entire creation as a manifestation of one central Cause? Could we love the individual unless we have some inner awareness existing prior to the advent of the individual?

The possibility of love existed before its expression or it never could have evolved. The greatest lovers have ever been the most God-like. If we would look for a God of love we must look long and deeply into each other. We must look away from the differences until we penetrate into the Unity of the Whole. Love alone reveals love. Hate but hides the gleam.

Depression and sadness do not reveal a universe of joy. We betray our spontaneity to the traitor of indifference and cry aloud that enthusiasm is dead and hope gone. The zest of life loses its keen edge to the coldly analytical. Mathematics may be necessary in computing distances or in counting marbles, but mathematics alone will never fire the heart of the average person with the joy of imagination. The laughter of the universe is not heard when the blood is cold. Warmth and color respond to their own and take no cognizance of their opposites. If we would know a God of joy, we must become joyful.

[handwritten: I FIND WHAT I AM TRULY LOOKING FOR]

God is distant to the unbeliever, unknown to those who are not acquainted with Him. The Spirit may court us, but if we would be wed we must first be wooed. There is no marriage without both bride and bridegroom and mutual consent. The prophets of every age have declared the unity of God and man, but they have been among those who have "entered in." Dare we deny the reality of their experience, the truth of their message?

[handwritten: NATURE IS ONE WITH MY NATURE]

We would have peace, but we still persist in remaining in confusion. The one is the opposite of the other. Cosmos does not affiliate with chaos. Some find peace while others find only confusion. We shall yet learn that each finds what he is truly looking for.

If we would find the more abundant life, we must live more abundantly. Life cannot be separated from living and whatever the nature of God or Life is, this nature must be one with our nature, else how could we be? When we enter into the spirit of livingness, we enter into the Spirit of God, for Creator and creation are one, Life and animation are latent in all things. When the creative power of our imagination stirs this latent energy into action there is a responding chord struck in our everyday experiences; we find that we are surrounded by Life. Truly did the great mystic proclaim that "he is not the God of the dead, but of the living: for all live unto him." If God is Life, and if Life is God, and if

God and Life are one and the same thing, how can we expect to become conscious of immortality while we contemplate death? All are eternally alive unto the creative Spirit of the universe. The persistent urge to express is a continuous demand which the original Life makes upon us. It is God, the Essence, passing through the thinker into action.

How can we expect to find beauty if we contemplate only unloveliness? The God of beauty is understood by the artist who appreciates the beautiful and senses in all form some reflection of that universal Wholeness which finds harmony in the perfect adjustment of Itself to all of Its parts. Beauty, like greatness, is a thing of the soul, a spiritual quality, outlined in form, objectified in space. It is eternally imaged in the mind.

God must be Truth. The Universe could not lie to Itself. "Truth, crushed to earth, shall rise again." If we would understand God as Truth we must be truthful. The lie is a mask, a masquerade. The irresistible desire which all people have to find the good life arises from an intuitive perception which already knows not only that God is, but that God is present with men.

The kingdom of heaven must be a state wherein one senses his unity with Good, the unity of all people with Good. This kingdom is as distant from us as is our sense of isolation from it. It is as near to us as our belief and corresponding act will permit. The kingdom of heaven is not a place, but a state of consciousness. God is not a person, but an essence, and man proclaims that this essence and atmosphere is personal, and so it is, but in this way: personal *to* us *through* us.

Each person in this sense may approach ultimate Reality and say: "To me It is personal, through me It is personified." The sense of the necessity of some mediator between God and man finds its answer in the responsiveness of our own soul to the universal Perfection. The mediator is our own belief, our own thought, our own conviction, our own action. As the mind cannot isolate itself from itself, or separate itself from itself, so it cannot inject into itself a mind which is not itself, or which is unlike itself, or which is other than itself. Hence it is written: "I myself am heaven and hell."

The mediator or savior which all people have felt a need of is already within. The only thing standing between the essence and atmosphere of the Spirit and Its personification through man, and in creation, is recognition. The fruits of right belief have always fallen from the tree of faith.

We need have no superstition about the results of prayer, faith, or inner awareness. This is the way the Universe responds to us, and the response is in accord with Law, for the Universe is built on the action of immutable Law. How far or to what extent we may prove this depends upon our ability to believe and to receive.

2 .

A New Faith

People are instinctively religious. By instinctively I mean that we are born with a religious sentiment. But many will declare that this instinctive religious concept is based on fear, that people have always been afraid of the unknown and have sought to propitiate it. Perhaps many of our religious ideas are the result of fear, but it is unthinkable to suppose that a sentiment which is universal in the human mind, and which rises in the intellectual scale with the evolution of the intellect, can be a delusion. After all, is it not true that instinct may be interpreted as one of the avenues through which the Spirit reveals Itself to us?

It is entirely possible, on the other hand, to say that many forms of religious worship are the result of mistaken concepts of the nature of Reality or God. It seems, however, a dangerous thing to take a man's religious convictions away from him unless one is in a position to give him better ones. It would be foolish to remove the underpinning from a house without first putting in a better one.

Fortunately our approach to Reality and to the religious sentiment need not rob anyone of his faith, but should give him a justification of it. I am not in sympathy with the idea that everything our forefathers believed was wrong. Neither am I of the opinion that we must believe exactly as they did. Any new form of religious belief will always be as nearly like the old as it possibly can be, but with the addition of new ideas. The transition is never too great. The impossible situation created in a nation like Russia today cannot last. We cannot compel a nation to become atheistic, because people are not atheists at heart. The heart already knows that some supreme Presence exists.

Not only do we instinctively believe and sense such a Presence and Intelligence, but everyone, insofar as he senses It and believes in It, finds a compensation for that belief in his own thought and he will not allow himself to be robbed of it. The religious sentiment itself will rise triumphant over any attempt to discard it. There is a Reality in this sentiment which we did not place there, but which we can draw upon. The problem which confronts the world today in the evolution of its religious concepts is not a problem of doing away with religion. Anyone who thinks he can do that does not think straight. It is not a problem of doing away with religion, but it may be a problem of doing away with certain dogmatic concepts which have been held by theology.

We cannot believe that God favors one nation or one person more than another. Such a belief degenerates into the worship of a tribal God. God is Light, and insofar as any man enters the Light, he will receive illumination. Thus the Spirit responds to each and to all at the level of the consciousness of each and all. Some psychologists will tell us that the apparent answer to prayer is the result of a subjective release in our minds when we pray. And I believe that in a certain sense they are right. Just as I believe that the confessional in the Catholic Church should never have been taken out of the Protestant Church, because it provides a release of the burdens of the soul. But there are many, on the other hand, who have not had any sense of the burden of sin. These people also have had some kind of response from the Universe which is difficult to explain on a merely psychological basis. Many believe that there is a communication of their own soul with the Over-Soul of the Universe. And we cannot brush aside their evidence or their experiences with a gesture of contempt.

The act of prayer is an attempt on the part of an individual to communicate with the Universal and to sense a reciprocal action on the part of the Universal. Now we can either do this or we cannot. If we cannot, there is no use trying. If we can, it is a healthful and happy exercise, both for the intellect and for the soul.

I assume that we can commune with the universal Mind and that It responds to us. If It can, then It must. I believe that it is Its nature to eternally express Itself through us, that it is Its nature to respond to us. It is Its nature to enter into us. The approach to Spirit, then, must be an approach to Something which desires such an approach, and to Something which responds to that approach. I do not believe that Spirit can refuse a man's approach to It. Spirit must respond if we approach It rightly.

It may be that our whole trouble is in the wrong approach. How does Spirit respond? If we are surrounded by an infinite Intelligence, how does this infinite Intelligence impart knowledge to us? It cannot do so externally, for the only way Intelligence can impart knowledge is by causing that knowledge to be known in our own minds. The only way that infinite Wisdom can become human knowledge is through an impartation of the infinite Wisdom through the human as knowledge.

Now, the Infinite is the sum total of all things, past and present, and must contain the potential possibility of every new thing and of all future knowledge. God, or the Infinite, contains within Himself or Itself all knowledge, all wisdom, and all instruments of knowledge and wisdom; hence, if the Infinite is one and indivisible, any instrument that It uses is simply some part of Itself.

How as individuals are we going to approach the Spirit unless we do so consciously? I cannot believe that there can be any formula given for this practice. The approach to Spirit should be direct and there should be an acceptance in the mind that there will be a direct response. Life and Intelligence is everywhere. There is no more or less of It here than there is in any place else in the Universe. There is no place where God is not.

A spiritual mind treatment—effective prayer—is for the enlightenment of the mind that the mind may directly receive; it is for the enlightenment of the consciousness that the consciousness may sense its spiritual existence. We all have a sense that there is Something bigger than we are in the universe. The average person at times senses himself to be an extension of It. I have never yet known anyone who did not at times sense a transcendent something. It is the Spirit in us, and our sense of this inner Spirit expands the consciousness, heals the body, and brings a betterment of circumstances in our experience.

The conscious approach to the Spirit is first a matter of

faith. The mind cannot contain that which it rejects, it cannot demonstrate that which it refuses to accept, and I think right here lies perhaps the crux of the whole matter. The response of the Spirit to us must be equal to our faith in It. It is always reciprocal, always mutual; the response is by correspondence, as a man beholds the image of his face in a mirror. The Spirit is a mirror before which we hold our minds with all of their thoughts, beliefs, fears, and faiths. The mirror reflects back to us an exact likeness of that which is held before it. How then shall we generate faith? Here is where a knowledge of Science of Mind serves us. Faith is a mental attitude and can be consciously generated. The Spirit works by Self-pronouncement, never by denial. Its words are *Yea* and *Amen.* We must learn to live affirmatively. This is the secret of success in using the creative power of our thought affirmatively. At times we deny the necessity of the reality of that which ought not to be, and we make this denial in order that the mind shall the more readily affirm that which ought to be. The denial brushes aside a false affirmation. But more and more we shall learn to "believe" constructively, to think affirmatively. For our thoughts and beliefs constitute our prayers to the Spirit.

We should learn to live by faith, but we must first learn how to have faith. And if we shall strip the idea of all mystery we shall soon discover that faith is a complete mental acceptance, an unqualified agreement with an idea. We can consciously generate faith and progressively demonstrate the supremacy of spiritual thought force over apparent material resistance, but not while we concentrate on the material resistance and fear it. Hence we must overcome fear by the denial of its power. We must generate faith by the affirmation of its presence. We must have faith in faith, and overcome fear by the presence of faith.

Quiet the mind and definitely state that faith and understanding are present. Mentally state and spiritually feel that a conscious and constructive Presence pervades all life. Affirm that the Spirit wills to respond and that It does respond. Sit quietly and believe. Now state your desire as simply as possible, using only such words as have a real meaning to you. Never try to use other people's thoughts. You are alone with the Cause; see to it that no denial of this thought enters your mind. As simply as you can, create a definite acceptance in your mind that you are being guided into paths of peace and abundance. Feel a response in your thought. Feel that what you state is the truth about yourself. *Affirm that you accept and believe and receive.*

3.

A New Universe

A pronouncement of one of our greatest modern scientific men, Sir James Jeans, was that we are coming to think of the universe as though it were an expression of an infinite Thinker, thinking mathematically. Coming from such a person that is a very interesting concept. What does such an interpretation of the universe mean from our point of view?

We believe there is a Spirit in the universe—an infinite, spontaneous, self-knowing Spirit. All religions believe this. Most philosophies believe it, and in the scientific world the opinion is divided. This infinite and spontaneous awareness we call Spirit or God—the universal Intelligence. We believe that there is also an infinite Law in the universe which obeys the will of this infinite Intelligence, a Law which cannot argue, which is intelligent, but unfeeling and unthinking. It is a Law which knows not why It does, but knows how to do what It does—an infinite Law which is mathematical in Its operation.

We very carefully differentiate between the Law, or the infinite Doer, and the Spirit, or infinite Knower. The knowingness of the Spirit we call contemplation or the word. That which the Spirit knows becomes the Law of Its action and this is the way Its Self-contemplation is manifest. The Law, being unfeeling, does not care if a man is a saint; It does not worry if he is a sinner. The laws of physics work alike for all men. Jesus, who was a profound thinker as well as a spiritual genius, announced this when he said: "Your Father . . . sendeth rain on the just and on the unjust." The Law operates according to the way It is contacted or used, and acts with precision but without emotion. But back of this Law there must be an infinite Emotion or else we could not have emotion; infinite Feeling, or else we could not have feeling; infinite Spirit or Being, else we could not be. The Spirit will never produce anything unlike Itself. Consequently, the very fact that we have warmth, color, emotion, and initiative, some powers which are conscious, and others autonomic, is all the evidence that one needs, if he be a rational and clear thinker. Back of everything is an infinite Mind or Knower!

Science is making a tremendous contribution in that it is deducing a scientific philosophy which will build up rather than destroy man's belief in God. Science has done another thing: it has theoretically dissolved the material universe. Science is sense, so it does not deny that any particular object or form, as such, is real. It has done away, however, with the material universe as a thing of itself and found that it is only energy and lines of force combining for the specific purposes of producing forms, all of which are temporary. It is interesting to note that the Bible affirms this position, saying that nothing is permanent in the objective world, that everything is in a state of continuous flow. Sir Oliver Lodge brought out this same thing by saying that the material form is always flowing and the apparent continuity of it is not occasioned by the flow, but by the mold which holds the flow in place.

Science teaches us that there is not an atom of our physical being that was in it even a few months ago. We can say this: We were born anew in this day and will be born anew in the next. A year from today, if we were to return to the same room we are now in, except for the mind that brings us here we would not bring anything with us in our physical bodies that we have with us right now. I do not see any reason, theoretically at least, why a person could not heal himself of anything, given time, if a new mold could be furnished. That is not just a metaphysical abstraction. The Bible says: "Things which are seen were not made of things which do appear." What we see comes out of what we do not see.

This is exactly the position that modern philosophers take; it is called the theory of emergent evolution, which means that when nature needs something, it demands it of itself, and out of itself makes it. So, in the evolution of the human being, when it was necessary for him to grasp, fingers were produced. Why, then, if it is necessary for you and me to know something we do not know, can we not—according to this theory of emergents—demand the information of ourselves and have it come to be known? The Bible says: "There is a spirit in man: and the inspiration of the Almighty giveth them understanding." Science, philosophy, metaphysics, and religion, viewed from the universal viewpoint, are all of much the same opinion.

We believe that when the human mind, individually and collectively, needs a new truth, out of the necessity of the desire comes the truth it needs. Everything we know in philosophy and science proves it. Out of the desire for a greater good come ways and means for creating the greater good; and if every person made a demand upon Intelligence for the solution to the present world problems, through the minds of those people who are our national leaders would come an adequate and happy solution. That is in line with what we know about the way Life works.

We must be practical; we must prove this modern philosophy, for unless we do it is worthless. We are conscious of certain needs. We need greater happiness, more love, wider friendships, deeper understanding, wiser counsel and advice, happier environment, a more tranquil mind, a healthier body. We say: "I have all these things; I am surrounded by friends, love, happiness, and abundance, my environment is right and harmonious," and this is what we call a spiritual mind treatment. By making these affirmations and believing in them, they possess the law of their own fulfillment out of the great universal Law. Our claim, being one of faith and belief, would call forth or cause to be manifested the answer.

Metaphysical practice is not the use of will power, nor is it an exercise to develop the will to the extent that one can concentrate on a given thought or object for some period of time. That kind of will, though popularly thought of as attending metaphysical practice, is contrary to the way in which Life operates. We use the will merely to decide what it is we are going to do.

Spiritual thought force is greater than any material resistance, because there is no material resistance to spiritual thought force. This is the meaning of the new universe—the universe explained as a spiritual system, a Divine order, a unitary and everlasting and indestructible wholeness, so near, so close to us that every thought form carries with it the cause of its own manifestation. So marvelous is that freedom which Divinity has bequeathed to us that it becomes our very bondage when we see it as bondage. It is our good when we use it as good. We have reached the place in our evolution where we can consciously cooperate and demonstrate the greater good.

Where is the individual's place in the universe? The universe cannot be a joke, yet it cannot be overserious. We become too serious, too tense. The universe is a joyous manifestation of some Self-sufficient Cause, some universal Intelligence, some Divine and ever-present Will and Purposiveness which appears to desire Self-expression that It may enjoy what It knows Itself to be. Man is Divine because there is imparted to him and incarnated in him some part of that indivisible Wholeness which is what we mean by God or Spirit. Every individual is some part of the universal Wholeness, yet each is unique in that no two people can ever be alike, for Spirit is eternally individualizing, personifying Itself in infinite variation while ever remaining a unity.

This is a stupendous concept, and when rightly understood will answer a great many questions. We wonder why there is suffering in the world—an apparent negation. If a man does the best he knows, if he is as good as he knows how to be, why is it that what we call ill-fortune can come to him? I think that everybody somewhere along the line must ask that question of himself, but it seems that we are now beginning to find the answer.

If we are made out of this universal Wholeness, then we are some part of the Divine Being and Its nature is incarnated in us, with the prerogatives of that nature—the power to do, will, and choose, the necessity of being an individual with self-choice, in which case there must be a Law backing up our choice. Consequently, we can bring to ourselves what we call limitation by the very same Law that could bring to us freedom. If this were not true it would mean that there was a law of freedom and a law of bondage—two opposing forces, hence no Infinite or Eternal. Jesus understood this completely, for he said that when man is in league with this infinite Purpose and Will, then It is he; the two are one.

Self-realization comes to us, not by antagonizing or fighting other people's ways of believing, not by struggle or by strife, but by recognition; that is, by knowing the truth, by alignment with the nature of Reality which is wholeness and unity, goodness, truth, and beauty. Self-realization is not a struggle for personal attainment; it is not the setting up of adversaries to knock down. As we come to the recognition of what and who we are, we will see that we do not have to contend with anything on earth. We do not have to strug-

gle to find a place for ourselves in the universe. In the sight
of the Spirit, which is also in the sight of our own spiritual
natures, we are part of Its expression, no matter where we
are. Anything that expresses is the light that It expresses.

This should add a new dignity to our concept of ourselves; it should enable us to know that that eternal I Am in
us will always remain infinite, unique, eternal, and yet, in Its
oneness, the root of all life. No longer does a man need to
feel himself to be a worm of the dust, a lost soul. There is just
as much God in one man as there is in another. If it seems as
though there were more God in one man than in another
it is simply because some men have used more of this Divine gift.

It gives us a new sense of human values to realize that
all humanity is Divinity waking up to Itself through self-
discovery and self-realization. Plotinus said that all men
have the kingdom of heaven within them. All men are of
God. Emerson said that all men are a part of the universal
Mind, and that all men are the inlet and may become the
outlet to the same, and to all of the same. Which is what
Jesus meant when he said: "I am the way." He did not mean
the limited Jesus, but the limitless Christ. He was referring
to the Divine nature of every man, that Divinity which we
come to in our own natures, that which is called the secret
place of the most High. "He that dwelleth in the secret place

of the most High shall abide under the shadow of the Almighty." It means the Divine incarnation, that thing which quickens by Its glory every act of our human experience. The greatest evidence we have of Divinity is humanity.

All our study and concern with theories is only that we may prove and practice them. Practice, then, is the art and the act and the science (art because it is harmonious, a thing of perfect harmony; act because it is an aggressive, conscious thing; science because it is subject to exact laws) of bringing our thought consciously and subjectively to absolutely believe and accept and embody statements and declarations which affirm the great realizations of spiritual perception as now present in fact, in experience and manifestation.

Practice is not suggestion. We would not suggest that God be omnipotent. Practice is not a rite of concentration, because we could not concentrate God. We do not try to concentrate livingness; we try to center our attention upon it, that we may see that it is concentrated already. Practice is knowing the truth that the same pure Intelligence—the volition and will that created the universe—is incarnated in us right now. The spiritual mind treatment becomes a statement of our belief, an affirmation of our investigation, and the specific things we accept in our treatment externalize in exact mathematical ratio as the beliefs which deny them are dissolved from our consciousness.

Ernest Holmes

We are not religiously superstitious. We say this: There is such a thing as Spirit. Spirit is intelligent; It is all-powerful. Spirit is really here; It does work, but It can only work for us as we let It. We only let It as we believe and embody It. Therefore, we will practice our belief. In such degree as we do this, we find that we are practicing self-realization, and this is the most remarkable thing that has been discovered: the power of spiritual thought force over apparent material resistance. The kingdom of heaven cometh not by external observation, but by internal recognition.

4 .

A New Freedom

I n the rapid evolution of the thought of our times we hear a great deal about superstition and Reality. Some claim that the entire intellectual edifice upon which the religious thought of the world has been built is a false premise and that our acceptance of it is superstition. While others claim that the principal trouble with the world today is its lack of faith in some invisible Power of Good responding to the petitions of mankind.

Let us define superstition and Reality. By superstition we mean any belief which holds that there are powers, presences, or intelligences of a universal nature which respond more quickly to one person than to another. By Reality is meant the nature of ultimate Truth. It is self-evident that we know but little about the nature of Reality. The scientist finds everything culminating in laws, the philosopher in abstract ideas, the artist in pure feeling, and the religionist in absolute Being.

But these differences of understanding and approach to Life are not as far apart as they at first appear. The apparent gap comes rather from seeking to approach Reality from one direction only. An impersonal and impartial getting together might show that the nature of Reality starts in absolute Being, impulsed by pure feeling, giving birth to ideas which operate in accordance with immutable laws. Indeed, an analysis of the situation seems to evidence this type of Reality and this kind of Unity. If so, we should discover that infinite Person does not contradict infinite Law, that absolute Will does not necessarily deny spontaneous feeling, and that the universal ideal of Truth and of Beauty must necessarily give birth to that which is both truthful and beautiful.

But to return to the superstitious approach: It is one thing to believe in infinite Will and Person, and quite another to believe that the will of infinite Person is more solicitous for the well-being of one individual than for that of another. It is one thing to believe that the nature of Reality is such that It must respond to us in such degree as we approach It in Its true nature, and quite another to believe that by petition It will or can change Its nature.

For instance, if the nature of Reality is wholeness, perfection, and completion, any expression of Reality must be wholeness, perfection, and completion. It is certain that Reality could never change Its nature or Its expression. It would be futile to ask God to be God, to pray that the Spirit of perfection should enter our being and make us whole, but to seek, through realization, to enter into the nature of Wholeness would be a true approach to Reality.

Emerson tells us that any prayer for less than the all-good is vicious. By this he means that there is no isolated good, no separated good, no absolutely individual good. He does not mean that it is impossible to individualize good, but that the individual mind is already a part of the universal Wholeness, which truth, when discovered and embodied, leads to Its proper manifestation—the wholeness of the individualized life.

We are born with the instinct to believe, to have faith, to expect and to receive. Whether we say it has taken endless generations of experience to produce this instinctive belief, or that the instinctive belief appears with us and that it has taken endless generations of experience to understand the belief, makes no difference. Just as it makes no difference whether we approach Reality through the laborious method of induction or accept it by the intuitive perception of deduction, we arrive at the same conclusion. Reality, to be at all, must be all and must include everything. Its process and performance may be and undoubtedly are through the law of evolution or unfoldment, but the Thing unfolding can never be anything other than what It is—complete to begin with, complete in all Its processes, complete in everything It performs.

Prayer is transmuted from a material and a superstitious basis in such degree as it seeks, through contemplation, to recognize the inevitableness of man's Divine nature, the absoluteness of his real being—not a being isolated from but included in a universal Wholeness. This prayer can be scientific, artistic, philosophic, and religious at the same time: It can be scientific in that it should realize the necessity of compliance with universal Law. It can be artistic in that it senses the impulse of original feelingness as the motivating power of everything. It can be philosophic in that it recognizes the nature of Reality to be infinite Intelligence operating from abstract ideal to concrete performance. It can be religious in that it recognizes the necessity of an infinite Personalness, an infinite and absolute Being. "For in him we live, and move, and have our being. . . ." It can be dynamic and effective in such measure as it has absolute faith and conviction that when it is true to the nature of Reality, Reality responds to it. It is impersonal in such degree as it realizes that Reality imparts of Itself alike to each and to all. It can be personal in such degree as it realizes that the nature of the infinite Presence is to express Itself, to embody, to personify, to go forth into creation. Thus the simplest fact of life becomes exalted, the meanest person Divine, and all creation the body of the Infinite.

The practical application of this apparently abstract approach to Reality is very simple. One should feel that he and all people are Divine, all united in one common Mind, all moving to one common end, the manifestation of this infinite Mind. And yet, at the same time, each can feel that he is a unique, a particular individualization, rooted in the same Unity but manifesting a distinct identity—forever the same but yet forever different.

Through meditation and by contemplation we arrive at the essence of the power of prayer, which is identification. Jesus said: "The Son can do nothing of himself, but what he seeth the Father do: for what things soever he doeth, these also doeth the Son likewise." He also imposed this condition upon Sonship: the necessity of entering through faith and acceptance into the nature of Reality.

A prayer for an isolated good, for a good which is to be enjoyed by one and withheld from others, cannot enter into the nature of Reality to such a degree as would a prayer which includes the all-good, which at the same time recognizes the presence of an individual good. Viewed from the meditative and contemplative viewpoint, based upon this concept of Reality, affirmative in its acceptance and seeking to become an embodiment of the essence of its own realization, prayer will yet be discovered to be the most dynamic force there is in the lives of individuals and in the destiny of peoples.

5 ·

A New Life

We sense in life a great mystery. There is not a normal-minded person who does not feel, for instance, that if there were something which could untie or loosen some other part of himself, there would result an entirely different manifestation of himself. I do not think anyone has ever lived, who has thought very much about the meaning of life and who has been willing to open his mind to interior convictions, who has not at times felt a bigger personality, a sense that this everyday individual is a projection of Something which stands back of it, projecting it. I do not mean the experience of a dual or a split personality. I mean, rather, the consciousness of a bigger self, the same self but more of it.

This is certain, the more deeply we penetrate the mind, instead of exhausting that which we are penetrating, the more we discover how much is left to be penetrated. We might have so much water in a reservoir and when we use it, it is gone; so much money in the bank and when we draw it out, it is gone; so much food in the larder and when it is eaten, that is the end of it. Everything in the objective world begins and ends in the duration of time. But when we enter the subjective world, the spiritual world, or the thought world—all of which mean the same thing—when we enter ourselves, we discover ourselves to be an inexhaustible reservoir. Why is this unless there really is an inexhaustible self which we all may feel?

The great problems which confront humanity today are not economic, not political. The problems of the day are those which deal with the soul and with the spirit. In saying this I do not belittle the economic problems, I do not belittle the international problems, but they are effects of man's mind. They are not causes. No government ever ran itself. No system of thought ever devised itself without the instrumentality of mind, of soul, and of spirit. Therefore, the things that we do, the things in which we are objectively interested are effects of our interior selves.

The real questions to which people are seeking answers are not like this: Shall I regain a lost fortune? For it does not make a bit of difference whether any of us regains a lost fortune. The questions which people are asking today are: What is worthwhile? What is it all about? Why am I? What am I? What, if any, is the reality of my own life, the integrity of my own soul? Is there any continuity of my own consciousness? Am I simply a happening in a universe which is chaotic, meaningless, destitute of intelligence and purposefulness, lacking in program and progress?

Today we are finding a transition in the race thought greater than at any other period in the entire history of the human race. The crumbling and the downfall of empires, the breaking up of established systems of thought, the changing of institutions, all conspire to cause the individual to look into his own soul.

This contemplation, this inquiry as to what it is all about, is producing a rapid evolution in our thought. Religious systems are changing. People are asking whether or not the church shall ever survive, whether or not any human institution can survive the terrific shock of recent years.

This inquiring attitude is a healthy mental state. The world, spiritually speaking, is in better condition than it has been because out of all this controversy, this mental turmoil, there will come some kind of an answer. That answer which is to satisfy the new order must do four things. It must satisfy the intellect, therefore it must be intelligent. It must satisfy our factual findings, which means that it must be scientific. It must satisfy our emotions, therefore it must be artistic. It must satisfy our cosmic sense, that is, the sense of bigness which the soul has, therefore it must be spiritual. The new answer must also provide a bridge between the intellect and the emotion.

Science and philosophy are things of the intellect. Religion and art are things of the feeling and of the emotion. Every religion which has ever been devised, crude as it may have appeared to a more cultured form of worship, has been an attempt to interpret in an objective manner that mystical sense which all people have. All the symbologies of the ages have been some attempt on the part of the intellect to interpret a spiritual sense which is instinctive in human thought.

We are on the verge of the greatest spiritual renaissance the world has ever known. Each one is seeking to reinterpret life to himself. There are certain things we must *know* about ourselves. Throughout all the ages there have been certain people who have plunged beneath the material surface and found a relationship of the individual to the Universal. We have called such people illumined. Always there have been people who, like Walt Whitman, have announced: "I . . . am not contained between my hat and my boots." That is either true or else it is not true. We will never know whether or not it is true by listening to what somebody else tells us about it.

Nothing can save the world from the terrible dearth of peace which is prevalent today but the soul itself. We may look about us for saviors but we shall not find them. We may listen to sages and can interpret or misinterpret what they say, but we will never find any satisfactory answer outside an immediate personal spiritual experience.

What is a spiritual experience? A spiritual experience is a certain interior awareness through which the soul becomes conscious of itself as being in unity with the Universal and with all other selves. We all have had such experiences in varying degrees, but is it possible for the average individual to have a satisfactory spiritual experience, so that he may *know*, so that he can speak as one having authority? The most pathetic spectacle in the world is a man who is not sure of himself. The most unhappy person in the world is the man who does not believe in himself. The most impossible mental state is that which does not know that good must come to all alike, at last.

We believe that there is in the Universe a limitless, all-knowing Intelligence with the infinite capacity to know and to be—an infinite, intuitive, instantaneous Power. It is impossible for the finite to grasp the full meaning of God. This infinite Being is, or has within Itself, what we may call an infinite personalness. This does not mean that God is a person as we think of a person. It does not limit the idea of Infinite to think that the Spirit has the elements of infinite personalness and the fact that It has produced personality is proof that It is possessed of these elements.

It is the nature of this infinite Being to express Itself. That is, It has infinite intelligence and feeling; It is an infinite artist and an infinite thinker. It is infinite feelingness; It has infinite personalness. It is the abstract essence of all concrete personality, the abstract essence of the possibility of the feeling of every artist. It is pure Intelligence—the abstract essence of the answer to every problem for It has no problems.

It is an infinite Will, not as we understand will, but an infinite Will from the standpoint and basis that It is infinite in Its capacity to know and to project. Therefore, the Truth or Reality is never a fragment. It is always a totality. That is what we mean when we say God.

This Infinite was, is, and is to be. I realize that the concept that I have given could produce absolute philosophic materialism because I could turn around and say that this Infinite has no beneficent purposefulness, that It is just blind, mechanical Mind. This may be an intellectual and a philosophic concept, but it does not satisfy us, mainly because we recognize ourselves as warm, pulsating, colorful beings. We long for human love and understanding and Divine relationship. The intellect, trained in things intellectual only, turns upon itself and destroys itself. We have witnessed such a turning in the world in recent years.

We wish to know if there is in the Infinite anything that knows us. We say: Does God know me? Every person is going to ask that question sooner or later. Either there is no Power, no Intelligence, nothing in the Universe that knows me or cares what happens to me, or else there is such a Power. We can no longer believe that we can pray to some God who will bless us but not bless our neighbor, simply because the neighbor does not believe as we believe. We know that whatever this Infinite Thing is, It is not a house divided against Itself. It is you and It is me, and It is all. But does It know you, me, and Itself?

I believe that the infinite Mind knows us but I do not believe that It knows us apart from Itself. I think Mind does know us but It knows us as a part of Itself; It knows us within Itself, not as separate or isolated. We are part of Its Self-knowingness. Therefore, I believe that our self-knowingness, what we know about ourselves that is really true is our consciousness of God at the present level of our evolution.

In saying this I hasten to add that I do not believe I am God. There is a great difference between saying I am God and saying God is me. Ice is water. All ice is some water, but not all water is ice. So we might say of the life of man: All

of the life of man is some of the Life of God; some of the
Life of God is all of the life of man; but man is not all of
the Life of God. It is my conviction that whatever my life is,
is God. There is no difference between my life and God in
essence; the difference is in degree. Consequently, if that infinite I Am in me and in all men is God, it accounts for the
fact that in moments of illumination we are able to see that
Thing back of us. That infinite Thing knows me at the level
of my ability to know It. Its Self-knowingness is me and my
self-knowingness is It.

There is an infinite Intelligence which gives birth to our
own minds, and if our own minds are in league with It, then
we arrive at the reason for the power of thought. The practical application of this metaphysical idealism is right here.
But there is likely to be great misunderstanding about this.
Mind is the thing that creates. My mind is the Mind of God
functioning at the level of my perception of life. Therefore,
to me my mind must be as God. It is the only thing that
could interpret, understand, accept, or reject. Because of
this, thought is creative. If this is true, and if this mind of
ours does partake of that universal Wholeness and is creative, then we are bound by our own liberty, and bondage is
an expression of freedom—man's freedom under the infinite Law of all life.

I believe that each one of us in turning to the great inner

life is turning to God. He who penetrates this inner life will find it to be birthless, deathless, fearless, eternal, happy, perfect, and complete. Gradually there dawns in his consciousness a sense that God, or the Infinite, is flowing into everything that he is doing. As individuals we must re-educate our minds, realize that we have as an ally a Presence and a Law in which the past, present, and future, and all people whom we call living and dead, live and move and have their being, forever unfolding.

PART TWO

The Creativity of Thought

Whether you realize it or not, whether you believe it or not, it is demonstrable that your thoughts are creative in and of your experiences.

This being the case, what your patterns of thought have been becomes a matter of great importance. In all likelihood you have been creating, without being aware of it, through the process of thoughts becoming things, many situations and conditions in your experience which are definitely not too desirable.

Any attempt to fully ascertain just why thoughts are creative is impossible. It is known and has been proved that they are. To go beyond this would be to penetrate the very nature and mystery of Life Itself. Although man's understanding of Life is increasing, the finite could never encompass the Infinite.

So there is a need to accept the fact that thoughts are creative, then proceed to think in the most constructive manner possible.

The following pages provide many valuable suggestions, ways and means, for the beneficial use of your power to think creatively. In your own mind lies the key that will open the door to the wealth of good things in life you desire, and remove from your experience all unlike them.

6.

Your Unlimited Possibilities

The possibility of this modern age existed at the time of prehistoric man. If there had been anyone then who knew how to build a gasoline engine and knew how to get gasoline, he could have had an automobile, so far as the Universe was concerned. In the evolution of his thought man provides avenues through which infinite potentialities can come into being. Man does not create anything except the form, the shape, and the use. Everything else already is in nature, and awaits man's discovery.

That is just as true when it comes to the use of Science of Mind. That is why I have often said that the practice of Science of Mind does not involve concentration or will power, as people think of those things. If it did, you could not use it. It is most amusing, but very pathetic, to see people concentrating on something, willing, trying to compel something to be. It does not work that way. The individual is merely providing the avenue through which That which is may express Itself through the terms of Its own nature. We do not will that electricity shall light a room; we provide ways for it to light the room.

The sooner we realize that this is true about the use of Science of Mind the quicker we will demonstrate its effectiveness. Nobody understands exactly what mind is. I don't myself. I just know enough about it to know that it is, and something about how it works. How it works is the most marvelous thing in the world; it is the greatest discovery that was ever made by man; it taps the greatest resourcefulness that has ever been tapped; and it works whether we believe it or not. The thing, first of all, is to believe it does. Some people can believe it does just because they are told it is true. And that is fine. It makes no difference how we believe it, or for what reason, but belief is essential. There is no approach to its use without belief.

If one can accept it in the simplicity of a childlike faith, that is marvelous. But if a person cannot believe with that childlike simplicity, he is not hopeless either. I have found that the people who come disbelieving and unbelieving and contradicting and arguing, provided they have good intel-

CONVICTION
ABSOLUTELY CERTAIN OF MYSELF

ligence, eventually have the best understanding. Conviction is what we need above everything else in the Science of Mind. I do not care if a man is the best philosopher who ever lived, or the most highly trained scientist or psychologist or religionist, there is nothing in the use of Science of Mind that will contradict any positive fact he knows. Therefore, we need not be afraid to approach the man who is full of "common sense." When he begins to understand it he will believe it.

We start with the premise that absolute Intelligence is fundamental. Just as I know I exist, and I respond to you and you respond to me because of our intelligence, Intelligence must recognize and must respond to Itself. The only way in which Intelligence can respond to Itself is by corresponding with Itself. That is why the ancients taught that Life responds to us as we respond to It.

Suppose we approach the use of Science of Mind with the desire of demonstrating success—and I am thinking of success from the broad-gauged viewpoint. A successful life must be happy, must be sure of itself, must be adequately provided for in what we call the material things, surrounded by as much beauty as it can appreciate, friendship which every normal person craves, and the experience of happiness and joy. There is no such thing as a successful person unless he is absolutely certain of himself and of his destiny. There is no successful life without the complete conviction of the eternality of one's own consciousness.

We must approach this understanding with belief, conviction, and flexibility. We are not flexible enough with life; we fight it too hard. It may be true that up to certain periods in our evolution we made progress by fighting, but after we have reached certain levels we shall make more progress by acquiescence. The Universe does not strain. It produces of Itself in peace.

We are surrounded by pure Intelligence and we are a part of It. Intelligence responds to us directly, specifically, concretely, and personally. God is Universal, Life is Universal, but at the point where the consciousness of man contacts It, It becomes personal. Therefore, when we approach this Principle of Life we should approach It not as something distant and far away, or something to which we petition. Jesus said: "Ye shall neither in this mountain, nor yet at Jerusalem, worship the Father . . . God is Spirit: and they that worship him must worship him in spirit, and in truth." He was talking to every living being. Therefore, it is not necessary that we go to some hallowed spot, to some sacred precinct, for Spirit is within us. We never can find Reality outside ourselves. Consequently, the one wishing to demonstrate a specific good must turn to his own mind and his own thought because his own mind and his own thought

constitute the place where he is an individualized center of God-Consciousness.

All we have to do is to state our desire, believe it, and let it alone. The hardest thing any man has to do is to learn to trust the Universe. We might say it should be the easiest thing to do, but it is not. We like to dabble with our request, pull our prayer back, give our spiritual mind treatment and then steal it back to see if it is taking root. In the last analysis a man must convince himself that he is in league with the only Power there is.

Someone will say, "Why is the world situation as it is today, and how can it be worked out?" It would work out this way: Everything is the result of intelligence and thought. All human conduct is a thing of thought acting itself out. Shakespeare said: "The thought is ever father to the act." When the majority of the mentality of the world agrees about anything, that thing always happens. If the majority of the people in the world were honest-minded, we would not have dishonesty. We will have what we call corruption and graft in public places until the minds of the majority of the people are honest, which time will not be while I would take advantage of you, or you would take advantage of me. But when that point in mind is reached we will not have any more dishonesty.

The Universe springs to the response of the individual

thought. But meantime there is no law in the Universe that says you and I as individuals have to wait until all the rest of the world catches up. "A thousand shall fall at thy side, and ten thousand at thy right hand; but it shall not come nigh thee." I believe that is true, otherwise we should be subject to a fate over which no individual would have control. The greatest power on earth today toward the stabilizing of the world is the individual, like you and me, who is thinking constructively.

We must come to the consciousness that Spirit wants to respond and does respond, and then we must accept It and accept It intelligently. What I mean by accepting It intelligently is this: If you will notice, you will see that everything in nature is definite. Nothing is chaotic. A seed always produces its kind. Even when there are definite combinations of specific things, the thing produced by the union of these two is another specific thing. This law of physics is also one of the greatest laws of metaphysics.

What we put into a spiritual mind treatment we know will come out of it, but we do not have to make the result. When we say we must put into a spiritual mind treatment what we want to come out of it, many people think that we must inject a positive force and energy against a reluctant force of nature and compel it to work. That is not so. If we put into the ground a corn kernel, we get corn. We do not have to make the corn come out of the soil. In fact, we could not do it. We only have to make it possible for the corn to be produced. If we had to put into our thought the force to make that thought effective or creative, we would be lost, for we would not know how to do it.

The one giving the spiritual mind treatment believes there is a Power and a Presence that responds to his thought. No matter what all the world believes, no matter what anyone says, he must believe that this Power directly and specifically responds to his word. As Jesus said: "Heaven and earth shall pass away, but my words shall not pass away." That is a conviction! First of all we must have that same conviction, and if we do not have it now, we must get it in the best way we can. I am not interested in the way. I am interested only in the fact that the way we choose shall finally get us to the conviction. We are to approach this Presence simply and directly and easily because It is right here within us. We can never get outside ourselves; we shall always be interior in our comprehension. I am here and It also is here.

Having reached this conviction, we state what we would like the Principle of Life to do for us. We do not wish a good for ourselves that would not be good for other people. But good is right; good cannot do evil. Abundance cannot hurt anybody. It is not going to hurt the rest of the world for you and me to have plenty. It is not going to hurt the rest of the world for you and me to be happy. Others around us need not think as we think; we do not have to watch the other fellow. There is nothing for us to watch but ourselves. We will never see anything or experience anything else but ourselves.

We believe all good is available to us. As much of that good comes to us as we are able to perceive. Therefore, in our spiritual mind treatment we must definitely remove the thought that the good we desire is not for us. Good always exists and disregarding anything to the contrary we can experience it. Everything that we do and say and think is based upon the infinite availability of goodness, truth, and beauty. Therefore, everything that we do and say and think should prosper. Our thought must come to believe it, affirm it, state it definitely and with faith until the mind comprehends what it means and is fully convinced of its own statements.

Then a thought comes to the mind which says: "But you haven't anyone to intercede for you, no influential person to make it possible for this good to come to you." Right here is where the mind must be alert and say: "This word has nothing to do with influential people. This word out of itself makes what it states." A spiritual mind treatment becomes a mental entity in a spiritual world just exactly as the kernel of corn is a physical entity in the creative force of nature which we call the soil.

The word which we speak in our spiritual mind treatment is complete and sure, and has the means and processes of producing itself at the level of our recognition of it. Consequently, as our recognition of our word becomes greater, the result in our experience becomes broader. We should work consistently and definitely to convince ourselves that we are happy, surrounded by an environment of goodness and truth and beauty, of friendship, of everything that makes life worthwhile. Our good is at hand. This is the day in which it is received, if we accept it.

When doubts, fears, and contradictions come up in the mind, we must consciously and definitely cast them out. We must remember that a thought is a thing. A thought that doubts good neutralizes a thought that affirms good, and vice versa. It does not matter what has happened or what condition exists. We must still affirm with an ever-growing conviction the active presence of good in our experience *right now*. We are dealing with absolute, unconditioned Causation right now, and in such degree as our concept embraces this conviction, we are able to demonstrate the condition we desire and eliminate our problems and troubles.

7

Using Spiritual Power

Let us define spiritual Power as the dynamic quality of that invisible essence of life, intelligence, and law which we call God or First Cause. The conscious use of this Power comes from the recognition that It actually exists, really responds to us; that we can directly contact and definitely use It. That there is such an invisible essence of life is evident throughout all nature, the visible side of which but proclaims this invisible essence. Objective nature, our own bodies included, is a phenomenon of the invisible Cause which we call Spirit.

Man is an incarnation of this invisible Cause, not by choice but rather by the Law of Life. As man touches his own thought, he touches It. He touches It with power, not because he wills this power to be, for *this power is.* This is the nature of the Universe. As Hegel said, the Universe consists of will and representation. This will is intelligent knowingness; its representation is creation. The will of Spirit, or the universal Will, must be goodness, truth, and beauty. As we imbibe Its nature, we come into Its harmony. The Divine does not come to us bringing an olive branch of peace with which to allay our confusion. The Divine knows no confusion. It persists in remaining true to Its own nature. The will of God *is* peace. Only the finite is confused; the Infinite remains certain of Itself. As we enter the atmosphere of peace our confusion vanishes. This is not done through objective power, nor by might, but through a realization and an embodiment of that Presence which transcends confusion. The spiritual Presence in the universe is real and dynamic. It surrenders Itself to us in such degree as we comply with Its nature. Our consciousness is so at one with the universal Law of Cause and Effect that when we know confusion we become confused; when we know peace we become peaceful.

Life never expresses by external impartation but always by a process of interior awareness. The very breath we breathe is God. We are not evolved from that which is unlike Spirit to that which is like Spirit. We are evolved *within* Spirit, by, from, and of Spirit. Hence, the very ignorance of the Law of our own being, while such ignorance continues, produces bondage. It is not as though there were a power of good on one side and a power of evil on the other. There is but one ultimate Power. This Power is to each one what he is to It. "With the pure thou wilt shew thyself pure; and with the froward, thou wilt shew thyself froward." The Divine exists to each only as a measure of his own belief.

The question arises whether any limit can be placed upon the possibility of the conscious use of spiritual Power. Theoretically it would seem impossible to place such limit. The only limitation would be that of belief and understanding. The Spirit Itself, in Its original state, must be ever-present with us. It refuses to change through any process of time. It refuses to be divided. Consequently, the eternal Wholeness Itself is immediately at the point of our perception—*all of It*. The question would not be, how far can Principle allow Itself to be used? but rather, how greatly can we understand It? Since Its whole purpose must be that of Self-expression, It must be Its nature to represent Itself spontaneously through our will, through our imagination, fulfilling our intentions, desires, or plans, for in so doing It finds Self-expression. The only limitation being that we must approach It in Its own nature. In such degree as we are in alignment with this nature, Its power must be ours.

If we could strip the mind of fear, superstition, and all sense of separation from this Divine Presence, approaching It quite simply and directly, we probably would be surprised at the results which would follow. How can we approach this Principle of our being other than directly through our own thought, and through a great simplicity of thought? What can a spiritual mind treatment, which is the conscious use of spiritual Power, be other than a direct statement of our desire and a simple acceptance of that desire? Since we are desiring, accepting, or rejecting at all times, whether we are conscious of the process or not, we are using this spiritual Power at all times. It is not alone in the moments of conscious self-contemplation that we use spiritual Power; it is in every moment of the activity of our thought.

Whatever condition we impose upon this Power causes It to appear to us as though that condition were real. There was once a man in America who healed many thousands of people through prayer. This man believed that God wished him to go barefoot, consequently he wore no shoes. It was necessary for him to go barefoot in order to arrive at certain conclusions in his mind. The Infinite did not impose this condition upon him. Could he have believed that God desired him to wear satin slippers, his healing ability would have been the same. Whatever this spiritual Power is, It works according to an exact Law of Its own nature. One of the accusations placed against Jesus was that he ate with publicans and sinners, that he allowed an evil woman to anoint his feet with rare ointment. How could such a man be holy? Yet he exercised a spiritual Power transcendent of objective limitations and proclaimed that it was through his belief that he did this.

Today we are seeking to make practical use of spiritual Law as well as of other laws. In order to do this we must maintain a spiritual freedom of the intellect; the mind should be free from dogmatic theological bondage, and we should come to believe that we can approach the Spirit both consciously and directly. Whatever spiritual Power is, It must operate through our minds, and It must do so according to our belief that It can do so. We should not waste time trying to discover what spiritual Law is, since no one knows, nor does anyone know what any law is—only what it does. We do know this, however, that in using spiritual Law the one having the greatest faith obtains the best results. It works best when we use It in a straight affirmative manner. Any method of procedure that conducts the mind to this place of faith is good. If the mind finds itself already there, then no method is necessary. If we really believed that we are surrounded by a spiritual Presence which responds to our word, that when we speak our word into It our word tends to take form and objectify, then we should have the essence of the whole matter.

The Universe is so organized, is of such a nature, that we reach this straight affirmative factor is such degree as we sense the supremacy of Good, the necessity of Good overcoming all evil, the availability of Good. The universal Mind is centered in Itself, knows nothing outside Itself, nothing different from Itself. It knows no separation. In such degree as we are conscious of this unity of Good, we are conscious of that truth which makes us free. Spiritual Power is latent within us but unless consciously used appears to have no existence. It is through our minds that we till the mental soil, cultivate and imbibe the Spirit, seize the affirmation of spiritual Power, and march with a surer tread.

Like other laws, spiritual Law should be aggressively used. As we come to see that spiritual Power is the use of a natural Law, the whole thing will become more simple. We shall no longer separate matter from Spirit, but will realize that we are living in a spiritual Universe right now, the Law of which is order and harmony, the Life of which is consciousness, and the Presence of which is both peace and perfection. It is said that God is Love, Reason, Beauty, Truth, and Wisdom—the essence of all salutary attributes and qualities—but if we are looking upon life with sadness, doubt, and fear, then to us God becomes these things, for if

Spirit should proclaim Itself It would be compelled to say: "I look at you as you look at me." This is why the enlightened have said that God's only language is *Yea* and *Amen*. This *Yea* is incarnated in us and our own *Amen* decides the form it is to take.

The transcendent powers of the human mind proclaim the Divinity of man. The more completely one penetrates the mystery of his own mind the more he must come to realize that he is not studying a human mind at all, but that, through the avenue of what he calls a human mind, he is penetrating an infinite sea of Intelligence. When we turn to that inner self we are turning to the Infinite. It is not our external personality but this inner Principle operating through us which gives us the power to stand and to walk, to think and to be. We must realize that there is no matter opposed to Spirit, no material universe separated from the spiritual Universe. All is One. We are not turning, then, from the human to the Divine; the Divine is but turning to Itself, giving expression to Itself. The *self* comes bearing its own gifts.

We lack the experience of consciously using spiritual Power because we have not tried definitely to demonstrate that we already have this Power and can use It. We must prove to ourselves that the power of our own word, spoken in harmony with the great Cause, is the law unto the thing whereunto it is spoken. When a majority realize this the thought of the world will be revolutionized and its objective manifestation will produce a greater freedom for all.

We neither fast nor feast to arrive at spiritual Power. Spirit is already in the loaf of bread. We are not spiritual because we refuse to eat it. Spirit already occupies all space, the loaf of bread adds nothing to It. The apparent power from fasting is not in the abstaining from food, but rather in the fact that the hunger for an idea is greater than the hunger for food. Some have fasted and obtained. Some have feasted and obtained. Both were right. Some have prayed without ceasing. Some have not prayed but have contemplated the inner Presence. None of these methods changes the eternal verities of our being. But, if any one of these methods causes the mind to more greatly believe and to more completely receive, that method is right for the one using it, no matter what name it may go by.

The Spirit knows Itself and knows us as Itself. It is only as we know It that we know ourselves. It is only as we embody this knowledge that we have real spiritual Power. What difference, then, whether we pray, sing, feast, fast, or dance? Only let us be sure that we arrive at our destination. And what is this destination? It is that place in our minds where we no longer doubt, where there is no opposite to Good, where God is all, but where God is natural, spontaneous—the interior awareness of our own thought. There will never be anything external to this inner knowingness.

The mind must definitely see what it wishes to experience and as definitely repudiate what it does not wish to experience. This repudiation is either through denial or by the nonresistance of nonrecognition. In the midst of confusion we must be peaceful; in the midst of fear we must be fearless; in the midst of doubt we must be certain. We must be poised and confident. We must expect the good and inwardly know that we receive, disregarding any apparent contradiction in our objective world.

Demonstration will be as perfect as is the subjective embodiment of thought. If we realize that form is Spirit in manifestation, that the father of any specific form is a subjective idea, and that we can consciously create subjective ideas, then we shall have a correct method for effective practice. The one wishing to make direct and conscious use of spiritual Power should first believe in spiritual Power and in the creativeness of his own thought. Then he should compel his mind to act as though his belief were true. When the subjective state of our thought, which is the inner mind, completely accepts an idea that is in line with the nature of Reality, then we shall demonstrate that idea in our experience.

All have spiritual Power but only a few consciously use It.

As time passes larger numbers of people will come to make conscious use of this Power until finally a majority of the race will be guided by that inner inspiration which guides men's feet aright. Then many of those questions which are now so perplexing in the social and economic order will be permanently answered.

8.

Your Word Is Law

The Universe is not only a spiritual system, It is an orderly system. We are living under a government of Law, always, whether we deal with the mind, the body, or the Spirit; whether we are dealing with physics or metaphysics. Although the Law is subject to the Spirit, this does not mean that Spirit is capricious and may create a Law only to break It. Instead, Law is always subject to Spirit, in that It is Spirit's servant, just as all the laws of nature are our servants and obey us insofar as we understand them and properly use them. The Spirit, being omniscient, understands and properly uses Law, which is part of Its own nature. Hence, Spirit never contradicts Its own nature, is always harmonious and complete within Itself, and exists in a state of perpetual perfection. While It always acts in accord with the Law of Its own Being, Its own Being is perfect and It never contradicts Its own Law. The Law is a willing and obedient servant; the Spirit is a gentle taskmaster.

We are of like nature to this supreme Spirit. We exist within It, having arrived at a state of consciousness whereby we can consciously approach It, believe in It, receive It. In recognizing Spirit we may use the Law which is Its servant, hence that Law becomes our servant.

We are intelligent beings living in an intelligent Universe which responds to our mental states. So, insofar as we learn to control our mental states shall we automatically control our environment. This is what is meant by the practical application of the principles of Science of Mind to the problems of everyday living. This is what is meant by demonstration.

Naturally the first thought of the average person is that he would like to demonstrate health of body, peace of mind, prosperity in his affairs; to neutralize a circumstance which is unhappy or to attract to himself some good which he has not been enjoying. Such a desire is natural and in every way normal, and the possibility of such demonstration already exists within the mind of every living soul. Every man has within himself the power to consciously cooperate with the spiritual aspect of his existence in such a way that it will create for him a new environment and a greater happiness.

But the greatest good which this philosophy of life brings to the individual is a sense of certainty, a sense of the reality of his own soul, of the continuity of his own individualized being, and the relationship of his apparently isolated self to the great Whole.

The greatest good that can come to any man is the forming *within him* of an absolute certainty of himself and of his relationship to the Universe, forever removing the sense of heaven as being outside himself, or the fear of hell or any future state of uncertainty. Man is a part of Life—some part of the eternal God. Man is forever reaching out, forever gaining, growing, expanding. The Spirit is forever expressing Itself through him.

Such an understanding teaches us that there can never come a time when we shall stop progressing; also that age is an illusion and that limitation is a mistake, that unhappiness is ignorance, that fear is uncertainty. We cannot be afraid when we know the truth, and the greatest good accompanying such an understanding of truth will be the elimination of fear. This understanding will rob man of his loneliness and give him a certain compensation in that sense of security which knows that Spirit responds by corresponding, a peace without which no life can be happy, a poise which is founded on this peace, and a power which is the result of the union of peace with poise.

We can be certain that there is an Intelligence in the universe to which we may come, which will inspire and guide us, and a Love which overshadows. God is real to the one who believes in the supreme Spirit, real to the soul which senses its unity with the Whole. Every day and every hour we are meeting the eternal and ultimate realities of Life, and in such degree as we cooperate with these eternal realities in love, in peace, in wisdom, and in joy, believing and receiving, we are automatically blessed.

It is not by a terrific mental struggle or emotional effort that we arrive at this goal, but through the quiet expectation, the joyful anticipation, the calm recognition that all the peace there is, and all the power there is, and all the good there is, is Love—the living Spirit Almighty.

A spiritual mind treatment is a definite act of the conscious mind, setting the Law in motion for the idea specified in the treatment. The one giving the spiritual mind treatment believes that his word is operated upon by an intelligent, creative Agency which has at Its disposal the ways, the methods, the means, and the inclination to make manifest his treatment at the level of his faith in It, creating those circumstances which would be the logical outcome of the ideas embodied in his treatment.

If we wish to demonstrate supply we would not say, "I am a multimillionaire," but we would seek to realize that

infinite Substance is limitless supply. We would say, "I am
surrounded by pure Spirit, perfect Law, Divine Order, limitless Substance which intelligently responds to me. It is not
only around me, but It is also in me; It is around and in
everything. It is the essence of perfect action. It is perfect
action in my affairs. Daily I am guided by Divine Intelligence. I am not allowed to make mistakes. I am compelled
to make the right choice at the right time. There is no confusion in my mind, no doubt whatsoever. I am certain, expect-
ant, and receptive."

As the result of statements such as these we re-educate
our mind, re-creating and redirecting the subjective state of
our thought. It is the subjective state of our thought which
decides what is going to happen to us and because the subjective state of our thought often contradicts our conscious
desires, a sense of doubt arises.

When we affirm the presence of good, any sense of doubt
is but an echo of previous experiences; it is the judgment
according to appearances which we must be careful to avoid.
For, unless we are conscious that we are dealing with a transcendent and a creative Power, how can we expect to demonstrate at all?

We must never lose sight of this Power. The demonstrations produced through the scientific use of this Power in

spiritual mind treatment are the result of the operation of the Law which is in no way limited to any present existing condition or circumstance. Evolution itself should prove this to be self-evident, and the one seeking to use this Power intelligently and constructively must have some sense and some inward conviction that he is dealing with an immutable, creative Law.

Why these things are so no one knows, but experience has repeatedly proved that we can use this Law. It is never a question as to whether the Law is able or willing, but rather a matter of our conviction that It does respond. The beneficial action of the Law in our lives is conditioned only by our unbelief.

The Law is both able and willing, and we might say that the only limitations It imposes upon us are these: The Law cannot do anything which contradicts the Divine nature or the orderly system through which the Divine nature functions; It must always be true to Itself. The Law cannot give us anything we cannot mentally and spiritually accept. In these two propositions we find the only limitations imposed upon our use of the creative Law.

But these are not limitations at all, for we do not wish anything contrary to the Divine nature, nor can we expect either Spirit or Law to make us a gift we do not accept. There is really, then, no limitation outside our own ignorance, and since we all can conceive a greater good than we have so far experienced, we all have within our own minds the ability to transcend previous experiences and rise triumphant over them. In order to accept our greater good we must raise our mental equivalents to reach the level of the good desired.

9

Accept the Good You Desire

The study of Science of Mind does but little good unless we make definite use of it. Science is the knowledge of laws and proximate causes. The technique of any science constitutes what we know about the principle of that science and our ability to definitely use it. A scientific truth can be demonstrated insofar as we understand it. If any particular theory cannot be demonstrated it is still in the realm of a speculative or theoretical science and may or may not be true. When a theory is proved to be true it should be accepted, and an intelligent and comprehensive way of approach to it should be given to the world. All people interested in that science should know that if they use its laws in a certain way they will be able to demonstrate its principle.

It is such an approach to religion that the world needs today, for all people are instinctively religious. Most normal-minded people believe in some kind of a universal or supreme Intelligence. Different people have different concepts of this universal Intelligence and react differently to It. We all feel that if we could only understand this God, this supreme Intelligence, and come into close enough relationship with Him or It, our troubles would cease to be. This has been the insistent urge, the dynamic vitality in all religions, because religion has ever been a way through which the human has sought to approach the Divine. Most religions have taught that faith in God produces definite results in human experience and it is interesting to note that in some measure they have been justified in their belief in the power of faith.

This at once suggests a "universal something" operating in and through all religions, for all have taught the possibility of communication with God, with the supreme Being; all have taught some form of prayer, and all have been justified in their teaching since through prayer and communication each has been able to demonstrate to its devotees that they are dealing with Reality. To those who no longer are interested in differences but in likenesses, who are no longer interested in negations but in the broader affirmations of life, there at once comes this thought: prayer and communion, stimulated by faith, have tapped some universal

Essence which has an actual existence and which responds alike to each and to all.

Without having the slightest superstition about the unique personality of Jesus as a man, I do feel that he either knew something we do not know, or he more completely believed something that we only *think we believe*. We accept theoretically what Jesus taught because it is beautiful, it soothes and calms us. His teaching has given the Christian religion the vitality that it has had; that vitality was injected by a few simple flashes from the thought of this remarkable man. Always there have been a few who have seemed to enter into his teaching, to accept it. Their lives have been attended by a spiritual and a mental magnificence which is marvelous. In going back over the teaching of Jesus, most of which has been superstitiously interpreted to a still more superstitious listening ear, what do we find? A most simple teaching—believe, and it shall be done unto you. What shall be done? The thing that we believe in, be it heaven or hell!

Jesus taught an absolute and exact equivalent and correspondent to the belief. When his disciples tried to believe—and how hard we all have tried—and were unable to do what Jesus had done, they came to him and asked: What is wrong? He answered: Have more faith. He told them to bring the boy to him and he would show them again. And they brought the one who was obsessed to him and he said to whatever was wrong with him: I command you to come out of him. And the boy fainted, becoming as one dead, but Jesus took him by the hand and raised him up and he was healed. Wonderful!

The thing that Jesus had done no other person could have done for him. He believed what he taught. We do not. We should not condemn ourselves, however, for our unbelief, but should seek to develop a greater faith. If one had the faith one could say to a mountain: "Be thou removed!" and it would be done. If we could only have faith it would be done unto us as we believe. This calls for a deeper search into the meaning of belief and faith, and when we are willing to take these two ideas, belief and faith, lay them on the operating table of the mind, dissect them and see what they are, we shall find that they are very simple; they are psychological, mental reactions of the mind to itself.

It must be that Jesus had convinced himself that the Universe responded to him, and that there was no lingering doubt. He came into such alignment with this universal Something that there was no longer any question in his mind about Its responding to him in the way he wanted It to. He said to the man whose servant he had healed: Go home, and when you get there you will find your servant well. That Thing which responded to him never seemed to fail. This Power did not say to him: "Now, Jesus, this man is really sick, he really has a cancer and it has been pronounced incurable." The Power responded to the great faith of this remarkable spiritual genius. It always responded to him since he never doubted It and because he lived in harmony with It.

There have been many others who have tried to believe. People have tried many ways, means, and methods—esoteric, occult, mystical. Most have failed. Occasionally someone has attained while the rest have proclaimed in awe: "This man has found the secret. If he would only tell us." And when he does, they say, "Oh, no, that could not be it, he doesn't want to tell us." And then they offer him a great price to be told what the secret is. They will seldom believe the answer. It is too simple; it could not be anything so simple as *belief* and *faith*, built upon assurance that Spirit responds to the mind of man *according to his acceptance.*

And so the endless chase for the secret goes around and around and around. The secret is belief and faith; expectation and acceptance, anticipation and recognition of the response of spiritual Law, Law operating through our belief in It. But how can Law respond while we deny the principle governing It? Can the mind accept that which it rejects? can it contain that which it pushes away from itself? Can any amount of intellectual endeavor do other than guarantee the maintenance of the convictions that the mind has affirmed?

We must return to a basis of absolute and utter simplicity. The way to use Science of Mind is to use it. The way to think about it is to believe in it. The way to demonstrate it is to act as though it were true and to stop acting as though it were not true. We must teach our minds to accept the idea that faith deals with the original Cause, the First Cause, the Thing that creates and sustains everything; to believe and understand that this Cause is immediately accessible, immediately flowing into our consciousness through the creative use we make of It.

We must give up our *unbelief* in order that we may entertain our *belief*. The one who does this the most effectively is the one who is not afraid of the external experience which contradicts his inward affirmation. He may acknowledge the condition, but he is at the same time conscious that the Power he is using is greater than the condition. The Power to do this already lies within every man's mind. It is already in you and in me, in Its fullness.

We must train the mind to believe. One of the first things that we must come to realize is that the Universe is not divided against Itself. The good we can experience is equivalent to as much good as we can conceive. Our well-being corresponds to as much well-being as our mind can conceive. When we give our spiritual mind treatments let us convince ourselves that they are *good* treatments.

When we declare that there is an infinite Intelligence governing our lives let us believe what we say. Let us spend our time in our spiritual mind treatment convincing ourselves that there is an infinite Intelligence governing our lives. Are we simply fooling ourselves when we do this? We would be if there were not a result attending such practice.

When a destructive thought enters and says you are just fooling yourself, you may be sure that it is just an old idea declaring that this whole thing is too good to be true. But we are dealing with a Power that actually is. And It will be to us what we believe It can be—no more, no less. Doubt will gradually lessen its hold until the time comes when it is as though it never had been.

Nothing is too good to be true! The best we have ever conceived is but a fragment of the whole Truth. We are surrounded by an infinite Intelligence, potential with all knowledge, which can, will, and wishes to intelligently govern our acts, for in so doing It comes into a greater enjoyment of Itself. The belief that a thing is too good to be true arises from the subjective atmosphere of our previous experiences which have so limited us that the fear of them maintains a hold on our unconscious imagination.

In spiritual mind treatment we do not argue with the old order of limitation, but seek, through a greater realization, to create and sustain in our minds a broader concept and a deeper experience. It is this belief and acceptance on our part that sets the creative Law in motion. Belief must pass through faith, into acceptance, by acknowledgment. As the seed is not complete within itself until it comes into conjunction with the creative soil, so our word must be buried in the infinite Intelligence, nurtured by belief and faith, watered by acknowledgment, tended with receptivity, and the outcome accepted with enthusiastic expectancy.

This is the meaning of entering into the closet and praying in secret, making known our request with thanksgiving, then the Principle which hears in secret rewards us openly. This reward is the demonstration. Do not argue with anyone over this. The way to use it is to use it, and there is no other way. Daily go into the silence of your own mind, saying, "Infinite Intelligence is at the center of my being. I am daily directed into paths of peace, joy, and prosperity. Everything that I do is quickened into right action. The Spirit of Truth goes before me preparing the way, instantly making perfect and complete the demonstration of Its presence in my affairs."

PART THREE

Thoughts
Become Things

There is a time for learning and absorbing knowledge. But then there must also come a time when such knowledge as you have learned must be practiced—put to practical use—or else it is of no value.

Faith without works is dead. Similarly, without properly applying the ideas you are absorbing your life will remain barren of the greater good you say you desire. Your thoughts do become things, so guard them carefully. Many valuable and practical suggestions are to be found here, but they have to be put to use before they will mean anything to you. In spite of how often or how much you may desire to turn to another for help in the matter of improving your life, in the last analysis there is only one person who can make you think the way you should, and that person is you.

A new experience in living, free from troubles and problems, lies ahead of you if you will but take the time and make the effort to do some proper thinking about them. Follow the suggestions for doing this that you will encounter, but remember they are but suggestions. You will have to take them, absorb them, and make them your own ideas before they will be of value to you. Then you will be able to loose the splendor that lies within you, and in so doing find yourself surrounded by all those things that make life worthwhile.

Your Spiritual Adventure

One of the greatest, if not the greatest, endeavors we could possibly undertake would be the discovery of the infinite creative potential that resides in our minds. In undertaking this discovery there are several specific ideas which can be followed and which, if properly used, may be productive of concrete and tangible experiences in our daily lives.

Suppose we wish to embark on a voyage of friendship. Suppose I am an individual, typical of countless other individuals, who is very sensitive, very confused; whose experiences have been such that I feel everything is against me and nothing is for me. Nobody loves me; no one considers me. I am quite conscious that once in a while I am asked to a party through some spirit of altruism on the part of another, and being conscious of this fact I am doubly miserable. I am that individual whom the world has apparently turned against, who hasn't a friend. Now I begin to embark on the voyage of friendship. The first thing I must do is to become friendly in my own thought. Not anywhere else but in my own thought. So I must begin in my own mind and say, "Everything is One. I have no enemies. I am one with all good. All good is one with everybody; therefore I am one with all people. Wherever I go, whenever I go, I am meeting friendship, love, kindliness, and consideration."

He who would have friends must be a friend to everyone he meets, must sense and know that everyone he meets is a friend. Whoever does this will find friends everywhere he goes. How long will it take to bring about such a desired result? It will take just as long as it takes. How will he know that his work is complete? When the demonstration is made. One is not healed until one is healed.

Suppose we wish to demonstrate peace. Absence of peace denotes fear. What is it that people are afraid of? Only a few things, and in the long run only one thing. We are apparently afraid of physical suffering, being misunderstood, lack, poverty, and the uncertainty of the future. But these are all the offspring of one central fear, which is that we are not sure of the *self* and the continuity of the *self*. I say in all

seriousness that the starting point of spiritual understanding, and whatever goes with it, is the solid establishment,
without superstition but by reason and such intuition as we
have, of the actual *beingness* of the *self*. That is why a great
Teacher said: "For what is a man profited if he shall gain the
whole world, and lose his own soul? . . ."

Our soul is lost when we are confused or in doubt. It is
lost when we are unhappy. The starting point, then, is one's
conviction of one's being as a manifestation of God. A man
cannot assure himself of the Reality of his own being until
he assures himself of the Reality of all people's being. We are
conscious of the real self which is established in perpetual
peace in such degree as we become conscious of the Universal Self in which all other selves exist. "For in him we live,
and move, and have our being. . . ."

To be conscious that one is poised in the Eternal, that
the outcomes of evolution are certain, that the continuity
of one's own soul is secure, that all is working together for
good, is what produces peace. There is no happiness, without peace, no true fulfillment of life, no real joy in living.
Peace is the pearl of great price for which a man will sell all
that he has in order that he may possess it. Peace cannot
arise from doubt or fear, but comes only in quiet confidence
and perfect trust. Peace is not in the wind or the wave, but
in the "still small voice." Peace is not to be found in the fu-

ture nor can it be dragged out of the past. Today we need to establish it as a mental and spiritual quality. It has nothing whatever to do with externals. We must arrive at the place of peace in the midst of apparent confusion or not at all. Not by the contemplation of the confusion, but by the recognition of peace itself, shall we arrive.

Self-treatment to know that "I am the principle of peace within me, which is God, the living Spirit Almighty," is desirable. In spiritual adventures of the mind we consciously use our thought to set creative Power in motion and then await with expectancy the desired result. We are, in a certain sense, experimenting not with Mind Itself, but with our own thought in seeing what use we can make of the creative power of Mind. This creativeness we do not inject into Mind; it is already there, a natural Law in the Universe.

We should each picture ourself and think of ourself as we would like to be. We should do this without contradicting the good of others, without seeking to coerce others. We should do this in as absolute a sense as possible, that is, we should withdraw from any contemplation of the relative facts in the case and think only of the desired outcome as being established in Mind. Mind finds Its own avenue and outlet and releases Its own energies for the purpose of Self-expression. Whether we think we are dealing with our individual mind or with the universal Mind, we are dealing with the same thing. What we call our individual mind is merely the place where we, as an individual, use the creative power of Mind.

Therefore, to "be still and know" means to get quiet in our own thought, to become conscious that the creativeness of the universal Mind is immediately present with us, to believe that whatever is in accord with Its fundamental unity is responsive to us; to believe that Its responsiveness is mechanical, exact, that any of us, no matter who he is or where he is, has immediate and complete access to this ever-available Power; to believe that It is omnipresent and come quietly to It, stating our proposition in complete trust—this is correct practice.

This great adventure which the mind makes in the realm of Spirit is perhaps the most fascinating thing we can do. We must be careful to differentiate between this form of practice and mere daydreaming. In daydreaming a person sits around longing for things, picturing himself as being something that he knows he is not, letting his imagination run wild, soaring, as it were, into realms of fancy. But in scientific spiritual mind treatment he does not do this. He takes a proposition which his mind can encompass, such as realizing that he is surrounded by friendship, right opportunity, and abundance, and compels his mind to accept this idea as now being a fact in his everyday experience. Consequently, his work is intensely practical, and although he is an idealist, he is scientific in his application of this universal Principle of Mind to the problems of everyday life.

What can be more practical than to set our mental and spiritual house in order and then, insofar as possible, let it produce for us the necessary things of life, the beautiful things of life? What can be more practical than to gain the ability to demonstrate in our experience that we can consciously call on a higher Power to do our bidding whenever our will is in conjunction with Its will, with the understanding that Its will never limits our real good?

You Live Your Ideas

When a man compares himself with others, he is prone to create within himself either a superiority or an inferiority complex. But when he identifies himself with the Universal, and all selves with the Universal, there comes a sense of unity with the Whole and he feels himself to be neither superior nor inferior. He sees himself and all creation as some part of God.

It is this identification of the individual life with the Universal that produces a true humanity. Righteousness and virtue cannot compare themselves with unrighteousness and vice. The Spirit knows Itself through Self-recognition. The devil is unknown to the great God. Good is positive. Evil is a denial of this good. The two do not meet. We should learn to identify the self with its Source, and this is the true office of prayer.

Cause and effect are inseparable partners, and when the self identifies itself with the Law of love and wholeness, through spiritual mind treatment, a corresponding effect in the outer life follows. This effect is an answer to prayer. Jesus called it a sign following those who believe.

A spiritual mind treatment or prayer should not be a petition. It should be a recognition. Most of our prayers are petitions, unconscious admissions that the soul is still passing through the travail of birth. We are not yet completely born into a consciousness of the heavenly kingdom. So we pray that God will make the crops good, that He will cause the rain to fall, that He will save the soul of some sinner. But whenever anything is wrought by prayer we shall find affirmation and belief—more affirmation than negation. God cannot work by negation.

Great religions are sustained by their affirmations and according to the universality of such affirmations they live and prosper. When the disciples of Jesus asked him to teach them how to pray he answered: "After this manner therefore pray ye . . ." and he taught them a prayer of affirmation. The method Jesus used was recognition, identification, unification, and then authority. He recognized a Presence and a Power greater than the human mind, but he did not recognize this Power as separated from, or apart from, the human mind. He placed it in the human mind—"Our Father which art in heaven." And he said that the kingdom of heaven is within. Jesus recognized the immediate presence and availability of Good and he relied on this Good in every emergency.

All great souls have sensed that the universal Spirit is greater than the human mind, but they have also known that this Divine Presence is one with the human mind. The kingdom of heaven is within. God is in His kingdom. The access to this kingdom is immediate and it will spontaneously flow through every man's consciousness.

Prayer, an act of the mind, is a recognition of the Divine Presence as universal Life, Energy, Power, Intelligence, and Substance responding to us. We need not feel that we must encompass the Infinite, for if we could encompass It we would exhaust the Infinite's resources and, being immortal, we should be condemned to an eternity of boredom. The Infinite will always remain Infinite, but It will always be revealing Itself to us in ever-widening circles of experience.

Through recognition and unification with Divine Intelligence the mind is directed; it comes to understand what the specific laws of nature are relative to any definite thing. The man of science is, symbolically, on his knees, listening greatly to the inner self, for it is through this individual self that we reach the universal Self. Those who have wrought marvelous things by prayer have been those who could stand still and listen. We talk at God too much, and seldom reach a place where we can relax long enough to let the great Self speak to us. God cannot listen to that which is contrary to the Divine nature. A prayer should be a mental and spiritual state of acceptance in the individual mind.

Where is the darkness when the light enters? Where is the lie when the truth is told? It is not, or it is as though it never were. It was only a supposition. The world has yet to understand that there is a great difference between a false belief and Reality, and that whenever Reality enters, the false belief tends to sink into its native nothingness. Jesus understood this, hence he told his disciples when they prayed to affirm the Divine Presence, to recognize It and unify with It: "Our Father which art in heaven, Hallowed be thy name"— a recognition that the kingdom is come. Great souls have listened to the Spirit; they have lived the good life of the Spirit, and the illumination of their consciousness has been a beacon light to future civilizations.

Prayer starts with this identification, this recognition of the Divine Presence, overdwelling and indwelling: "It is no longer my human will, but Thy Divine Will." True prayer does not affirm: "I will do thus and so." Who by affirming that black is white will change its color? We cannot expect any prayer to be answered if its answer requires the denial of any law of nature or a contradiction of the true nature of the Divine Being. But we can and should expect an answer to any prayer which is prayed in accord with the nature of Reality. In such prayer a definite, cosmic Force is set in motion through our faith, belief, and conviction.

It is because of this that the religions of the world have had their power, for with all great religions has come a spiritual conviction, an acceptance of an overshadowing Presence, and a desire to enter into harmony with It. Religion is not a thing of itself, but is an approach to the Thing Itself.

The Infinite does not contend with anyone or against anything. How seldom, then, are our prayers in accord with Its nature. We do not know the possibilities of the Divine Law, nor should we feel discouraged if we do not ourselves measure up to our highest sense of Its possibilities, but we should learn to have faith and to accept a continuously expanding good.

By certain laws of our own nature we may be limited and bound. By a greater understanding of these same laws we are free. The first steam-driven ship to cross the ocean carried in her hold a book, written by the scientific men of that day, explaining just why it was that a boat could not be driven by steam.

We do not know the possibilities of man, and while we

cannot believe that prayer will change the Divine nature, we can believe, without violating our intelligence, that prayer might awaken a deeper Divinity, a greater possibility, and bring into our experience a greater good. But the only evidence we have of our faith and its validity is in the result obtained.

We do not have to say that people are not sick in order effectively to give a spiritual mind treatment for their recovery, but how can we doubt that there is a Power inherent within all people to heal? How can we place any limitation on Its capacity or willingness to act in our behalf? The contemplation of the Divine Life, awakening within us a recognition of and a receptivity to Its influx, is the greatest single curative agency known to the mind of man.

We do not know what the energies of Mind and Spirit are. We do not even know what Consciousness is. Causation will not stand too close an intellectual scrutiny; It avoids the issue and, remaining true to Its own nature, argues with no man. All we can say of It is that *It is*. That the impulse of the Creative Genius starts in pure Intelligence, we must inevitably conclude. That Consciousness is back of all that lives, seems to be self-evident. That the universal creative Mind projects Itself upon the screen of Its own experience through the contemplation of Itself, I accept. That man is of like nature to this Mind is the teaching of the great of the earth.

Why, then, should not a man of the perception and spiritual intuition which Jesus had, living as he did in harmony with the Universe, declare that all things are possible to him who believes, if his belief is a true belief and in accord with the Universal purposes. Laying aside all differences of opinion, all theological controversy, and all philosophic abstractions, and coming down to the simplicity of the thing, we must learn to believe, to have faith, and to accept, knowing that as we do this we are entering into that Power which is not bound by any existing circumstances or conditions whatsoever.

We should learn to identify ourselves with right action, with pure Life, with perfect Intelligence; to unify ourselves with Good, and to contemplate right action as now being apparent in our affairs. It matters not what has gone before, for if we introduce a higher state of consciousness it will be made manifest in our affairs.

Well did Tennyson say that "more things are wrought by prayer than this world dreams of." Prayer contradicts no scientific fact, affirms no impossible state of being, contradicts no law of nature, but rises gently to the comprehension of the Divine Presence as an agency of good, of right action, and of immediate availability.

It is our privilege to prove our faith through our demonstrations. This we shall do through the contemplation, in our own minds, of the Divine Presence. Our life is created by our ideas, so in actual practice we must turn resolutely from the condition which obstructs and contemplate its opposite, affirming the presence of the desired result even in the midst of confusion, assuring ourselves that the Divine Presence is the Law unto our faith, bringing immediately into our experience the healing of our body, the beautifying of our circumstances, and peace to our mind.

Think Effectively

There is a great desire in the minds of all of us to feel and believe that each has within himself a principle, or a consciousness, or a way of arriving at peace, joy, and plenty. I am not going to say that it is possible to demonstrate a spiritual tone while we do those things which contradict the truth we seek to demonstrate. On the other hand, I do not wish to compromise our belief because we believe, and rightly, that there is a Principle which if correctly approached and embodied will work for our good.

There has been throughout the ages enough experience to prove this, whether we consider part of that experience as the answer to prayer or merely a psychological reaction. Prayers have been answered, of that there is not the slightest question. Many prayers have been answered, and many prayers have not been answered, in the experience of the human race.

We are confronted with a fact and not a theory. We seek to find a theory that will fit the fact. We must first have the fact and then evolve the theory. It is a wrong method to start with a theory and try to compel the fact to fit it. Such theory has been held among many right-minded, religious people. These people have tried to explain this and they have said, "Sometimes God feels that it is good to answer our prayers and at other times He feels that it is good to let us suffer a little longer." This has been a very sincere thought. Personally, however, I do not believe that it is a true thought. I do not believe that God wills suffering to any living soul at any time for any reason. It cannot be that way, for if God desires us to suffer, then it is certain that we are going to suffer and all the prayers, wit, and science, and all of the philosophy and religion will not stop that suffering because what Omniscience wills, It decrees, and what It decrees is inevitable.

The answer to the question why some people have their prayers answered and others do not is not in the will of God but in the act of man. That which is Life can will only life. That which is Freedom can will only freedom. That which is sufficient unto Itself can will only self-sufficiency. We need not bother as to whether or not the will of God is that we shall suffer. The poor do not suffer any more than the rich, but they suffer in a different way. The ignorant do not suffer any more than the intellectuals. From the popular concept, the bad do not suffer any more than the good. It cannot be that limitation and suffering are imposed upon us by the Deity. They are the result of ignorance. Insofar as we express ourselves rightly, in accord with the Divine harmony, the Divine Self goes forth anew into expression through us; we are avenues through which God comes more completely into fruition.

The Apostle James said: "Ye ask, and receive not, because ye ask amiss. . . ." I do not feel, as many people do, that a prayer for a personal good is asking amiss. But if our prayer is for a personal good which we would refuse to others, it is a prayer based on the belief that the Universe is divided against Itself. Such a prayer cannot disturb the infinite Unity and Harmony. But to suppose that one serves the Universe or society any better by denying himself good is to suppose that there is not enough good to go around. When we pray amiss it is not that we pray for individual good, but it is that the prayer contradicts the universal Good, the Divine Harmony. If we exist, we exist for the purpose of self-expression, fullness of expression, joy, and completion. We exist "to glorify God." But God is glorified only as God is expressed.

I do not think we need to have any theological tremblings as to whether or not we have suffered enough. We have suffered more than enough, so far as I am able to deduce. It must be that we are not quite in accord with the fundamental harmony of Life. I know someone will say, "Well, we have no right to ask for an individual good while there is want in the world." There has always been want in the world and there will continue to be until the majority of people think right and act right.

We may look at this proposition from the materialistic viewpoint and say that there is no beneficent God, no final Power or Mind in the Universe which cares. Or we may look at it from the standpoint of a sense of religious restriction and say that God does not want us to have plenty. But we will find that both points of view are wrong. As religionists, we cannot conceive that there is an infinite God who creates a world and countless numbers of people but fails to create at the same time the way for those people to express life. Since limitation cannot be part of the Divine scheme, we must arrive at the conclusion that the Universe is not against us; we are against ourselves.

Still there is the question: Why is it that some people's prayers are answered and some are not? The answer is in the prayer. There are times when our prayer is in accord with Reality and that prayer is going to be answered. In such cases prayer is always answered, whether it is prayed in the name of Jesus Christ, or Buddha, or disregarding all methods, it is a direct statement to God. If a man embraces these three concepts—the unity with Good, the belief in Good, and the receptivity to and mental equivalent of Good—his prayers will always be answered.

When a man says, "If you are doing the will of God you will prosper," he is right. But I would say to him, "How do you know what the will of God is?" The only way we can know what the will of God is is to understand the nature of the Universe in Its final integrity. It is Unity. Its purpose is to project life and more life. Consequently we must be in unity with Its Oneness, Its Life. It is ever present. We must feel that It is ever present. It is eternal. We must feel that we are eternal. We must believe that It is in us as we are in It. If we expect the Truth to make us free, we must understand what the Truth is and how It works. We must not expect God to give us anything that He would withhold from anybody else.

The Universe must be a unity, a harmony. If It is a unity, It has to be a harmony, and if harmony, It has to possess beauty and balance. The average person believing in good, willing everyone good, need not be afraid that his prayer is selfish. There would have to be something of a universal essence in his nature. If I cannot go into a Catholic church and kneel and pray, or into a Buddhist temple, I am unfortunate. The same heart beats in every man's breast. We must come into a Universal sense of things. Our own good is good for the world. If we feel that way, why should we feel that God desires to withhold any good? How can we *really* live while we feel that there is anything in the universe that is not included in the great universal Wholeness of things? Spiritual thought penetrates the past and future and finds the present but a continuity of experiences threaded on Something which of Itself is changeless. The will of God is obeyed when we are in unity.

And the next thing is belief. Jesus said: "When ye pray, believe that ye receive. . . ." He was announcing a Law which has an analogy in the physical life—when we wish to harvest crops we plant seeds. The physical universe in the last analysis is a mental and spiritual thing. It is Mind in action.

God is a universal Presence and a universal Responsiveness. God creates by Self-knowing. God does not doubt His own Self-knowingness. That is why it is that if we wish to use the Law of Mind we must not only unify with It but we must believe It. We must unify; we must believe; we must receive. We must receive into the mind because the mind cannot contain what it rejects. A thing, so far as the mind is concerned, cannot be true and false at the same time. I cannot speak a lie as though it were the truth. I cannot say, "I believe" and by saying it, believe. But if I really believe, I know that I believe. I cannot say, "I receive," if there is a doubt. We are trying to analyze the things necessary to assure the answer to prayer. What we know, we can prove. We want to know by having lived and proved.

We must believe; we can receive only an equivalent of what we believe. I am not in sympathy with people who say that everything is all right when it is not. The man who is confused cannot demonstrate peace while he remains confused. It is only as he drops his confusion and enters into a state of peace that peace abides in him. We must embody. Can anything emanate from us unless it is first in us? We must expect to be able to demonstrate or have our prayers answered today according to the degree of life we embody today. But we are ascending, enlarging, expanding all the time. Out of the experience of today we will know a greater good tomorrow and so there will always be expansion.

The Universe never disputes, contradicts, or denies Itself. It is not alone what the intellect announces, what the mouth speaks, or the conscious thought thinks. In the last analysis, it is our whole inward thought—what psychology calls the subjective state of our thought—which decides. And this is where the practice of Science of Mind comes in. If we say, "I guess God did not want me to have that good thing for which I prayed," this is the reason it is not always done at once. If the subjective state of our thought denies what our objective thought says, it neutralizes that objective thought.

In the old order of thought we had what was called "praying through." This does not mean praying through God, but through our own minds. It means praying until our conscious thought believes and our subjective thought no longer denies—praying until all doubts are removed. We do the same thing now, but we do not call it that. It is "dressed up" a little differently and it seems more intelligent, we think. When we say, "We treat," what do we mean? Spiritual mind treatment is a mental adjustment; it is doing something to the mind so that the mind no longer denies or refutes the idea which it embodies in a treatment.

A person should feel that he is surrounded by a creative Mind which receives the impress of his thought and acts upon it. He is in this Mind and this Mind is in him. The power by which he thinks is this Mind in him. His mind is not another mind, but that One Mind manifesting as the individual, as himself. Each of us, as an individual, evolving into reason and freedom, is continuously using that Mind at the level of our consciousness.

The greatest thing that has ever come to the world in the entire history of its evolution is the conscious recognition that there is a creativeness in our own minds which uses a Creativeness that is infinite; that each man in the integrity of his own soul can enter this universal Goodness and take from It as much as he is now ready to receive.

Build a New Life

The past is gone, yet the experiences of the past are written in memory, and memory contains the accumulated knowledge of the individual and of the race. We continuously depend on this source for information, for inspiration and guidance. Could memory be entirely extinguished, both in the mind of the individual and of the race, the entire background of our life would disappear, the stream of consciousness would be abruptly severed. No greater catastrophe could be imagined. It is inherent in our nature that memory and experience shape and mold our lives toward greater attainment and eternal progress.

Hence the time past is giving birth to the present time in which we recognize, understand, and experience the activities of everyday life. Recognition, experience, and activity slip away into the past, ever building a more substantial foundation upon which in time, now only anticipated, we shall rear a more noble edifice.

Could the expectation of the future be removed from the enthusiasm of our vision, all efforts of today would be futile. Life has instinctively provided that there shall ever be held before our waiting thought a goal, not too easily reached. Symbolically, the face of progress is ever toward the future, facing the light of the goal before it, while casting its shadows behind.

Since it is impossible for anyone to rob himself entirely of memory, it behooves all to guard carefully the experiences of the present that when they do become memories they shall be happy ones. It is a well-established fact, according to the known laws of the mind, that if one is retaining unpleasant incidents in his memory they can be neutralized through the power of his own word and his imagination. This is the secret of the confessional and of psychoanalysis—to remove the stain, the hurt, and the condemnation from the past, leaving in their place the gentle urge of better purpose and a sense of the Divine forgiveness.

If we are carrying about in our memory that which does not measure up with harmony, we should consciously discharge it, knowing that though all of us have made mistakes there is still no power in the Universe which wishes us ill. It is impossible to draw a fair estimate of the life of the soul from the short-range experiences of a few years. We are eternal beings on the pathway of experience for the purpose of gaining true individuality; even our mistakes are a part of our evolution and should be so considered. Let our present experiences be of such character as to harm no one and help all. Then shall the past be a beautiful memory, the present a glad hour, and the future a joyful expectation. All souls are eternal, all men are Divine, and in the long run good shall come to all.

From the viewpoint of infinite Mind it must be that what we call the past, present, and future are one. The Omega must be potential in the Alpha. Thus it is written: "I am Alpha and Omega, the beginning and the end"—he that was and he that is to come. The potentiality of our lives must have been forever in the Divine Mind, so as individuals we should forever expand, continuously growing into the likeness of that Divine Spirit inherent in all men. Could our eyes completely penetrate the spiritual realms, and could our imaginations rise by pure intuition to the comprehension of Reality, we should, no doubt, perceive what the illumined have seen and sensed: that there is very little between us and heaven, and that this is entirely bound up in our own concepts.

This intangible Thing which refuses analysis, this subtle Presence which can be neither caught nor bound, the Life

Principle and the intelligent Consciousness within us, partakes of the nature of eternity and cannot even conceive of Its own birth, nor can It possibly experience, even in Its own imagination, any reality to Its passing. Thus can eternity be crowded into a day or a day stretched forth into eternity.

In the study of Science of Mind we learn that the sequence of the creative order is: first, Intelligence; next, the movement of Intelligence as Law; then, manifestation of Itself as creation. Whatever the nature of the physical universe is—and no one *knows* what it is—it is certainly not an illusion. Creation, or visible form, is necessary to the life of the Spirit, for without it the Spirit would be unexpressed. As time is a creature of eternity, so form also is the creation of time, and both time and form are forever necessary to self-expression, whether considered from the viewpoint of the individual or the universal Life.

Let us never think of creation as an illusion, or of things as being evil in themselves. The illusion is never in the *thing* but always in the way we look at it. The infinite variations of life, the eternal manifestations of creation, though in changing forms, *all* point to the fact that the Infinite clothes Itself in form in order that It may enjoy Its own Being. It must do this through the power of Its own imagination backed by the Law of Its own word. There is no other possible conclusion at which we can arrive.

Man as the complement of the Spirit is of the image of the Father; partaking of the Divine nature he must also have an inherent power within which is creative. This creative power immanent in man is not placed there by the disposition of his own will nor through the imagination of his own thought, but should be considered rather as the nature of his being. In other words, we should not attempt to explain why ultimate truths are true; they are true because they are true. Having discovered them there is nothing left other than to accept and utilize them.

If there is any truth relative to the individual life which is of greater importance than this, it is that the thought of man deals with a creative Agency or Power. From this he can never escape. Our word, our thought, our imagination are all creative. We did not hang the stars in space nor set the lofty peaks overlooking the sea, but we *have* imagined unhappiness and we *do* experience in life the outward manifestation of our inward convictions. Thought is an actual force dealing with a potential creative Power in the Universe of which only this can be said: It is.

Our thought operates independently of conditions, and has the possibility of transcending circumstances as they now are and causing new ones to be created. However, we should bear in mind that the creative Power is only set in motion by our thought. The Power Itself belongs to the Universe, and no man made It. All that we can do is to accept It, believe and use It. But while we continuously remold thought according to the pattern of ancient ideas, we remain bound by previous opinion, bias, and prejudice. We must do something to break down the walls of experience and expand the vision of the soul. Here our imagination comes into play, enabling us to conceive a greater good.

Neither the will nor the intellect is creative; they simply decide what the thought, the emotion, and the imagination shall respond to. The one who would rise above previous conditions, transcend intolerable limitations and create a better situation for himself must deliberately turn, in his imagination and thought, from the old order, and with a calm but flexible determination, endeavor to contemplate only the good, the beautiful, and the true. He should refuse to admit into his consciousness any controversy or argument, compel himself to know and to accept that in the apparent isolation of his own soul, from the genius of his own thought, he is molding an individualized destiny out of the Essence from which all form emanates.

Suppose we could reach the place where we no longer contemplated adverse conditions, opposing forces, or divided power of good and evil. Would we not be at peace, our minds tranquil? Could we ever again be afraid? We lack peace because we have torn the Universe into pieces and set one part against another. The din and roar of the human conflict has so filled our ears with discord that we no longer hear the heavenly voices. Our eyes have become so blinded by self-grief and self-inflicted wounds that we do not even behold the harmony in nature. *Power* cannot come out of confusion. *Power* is the child of peace and poise, the union of which must forever give it birth.

Let us contemplate strength and forget weakness; let us meditate upon peace and poise, forgetting the confusion. The first step toward this goal is a realization of the integrity and the eternality of our own being, and of that universal Wholeness from which we spring and *in* and *by* which we live. From such contemplation comes the establishment, not of a self-centered life, but of a life centered in the eternal Self—not egotism but egoism.

What if our immediate universe does tremble to its very foundations? What if the "slings and arrows of an outrageous fortune" are apparently directed toward us, shall not our armor of faith shatter them in dust at our feet? Who can measure life by *one* experience, or estimate the possibilities of the soul by the slight observations of any *short* period of time? The soul knows no limits but finds itself eternally merged with the One whose only answer to man is *Yea*.

Abundance is a state of mind. The Universe abounds with good. The Universe must be a self-sustaining and self-perpetuating spiritual order amply able to provide for Its own needs, and adequately able to express Its own inherent desires. Man is some part of the Universe. Why, then, is he limited unless it be that he has contradicted the fundamental principles of self-existence, and, in ignorance of his true nature, repudiated the greater claim which he might have made upon the Universe?

Prosperity is a state of mind; activity is also a state of mind; and the law of compensation is an invisible but infallible government of Divine order. It is done unto us *as* we believe, but belief is largely subjective and we are all more or less marked by the grooves of experience, a large portion of which has been adverse. Those who wish to demonstrate the effectiveness of spiritual mind treatment must *claim and know*, in their own thought, that there is a Divine Intelligence directing them and providing the ways and means for their thoughts to become things.

All thoughts of doubt and fear must be resolutely banished from the mind. We must learn to build upon faith, live in a state of conscious receptivity and enthusiastic expectation. Let us no longer limit the future possibility of eternal progress in our own lives and affairs. We are living in a spiritual Universe and we should always remember that the Universe responds to us as we respond to It.

Live Creatively

A great many people are in some degree destroying their happiness because they have inner desires to create that are unexpressed, and these desires stifle them, congest them emotionally and physically, and make them unhappy.

There is a great deal of physical starvation in the world today, but there is a great deal more mental and spiritual starvation than anyone realizes. It takes only a short while to starve to death physically, but think of the people who have plenty to keep the body going but who are starving the mind and the spirit, year after year.

Back of every man's life there is a natural desire to express, to accomplish constructively. It does not matter what the accomplishment is. To the universal Desire Itself the creation of an empire involves no more than the building of a bridge; It does not know that one is great and the other small. All this inner Urge knows is what It feels, and It feels Itself to be. Because It feels Itself to be, It knows It has to express, and because It knows It has to express It beats against our consciousness, and that expression fulfilled is what we call self-expression.

A man who is self-expressed is always happy. He is not afraid of his stand, no matter what it is. This Urge does not know any comparison. If It did It would be confined by finite limitations. It just knows Its necessity to express. We feel this impulse. Even a child feels it. A child wants to do something, but the parents squelch that desire. After a while the child is inhibited and if unable to express his desire secretly will have a sense of having been repressed. Of course, on the other hand, we know that we cannot allow children to do exactly as they want to do. Therefore we say that there must be a balancing. The child must express but he must do it constructively. A child can be very easily taught what is constructive.

We are all just children of a larger growth, a greater experience, and sometimes a deeper perception. When we find that we have this perfectly normal desire to express, we must decide what we are going to express. The intellect must consciously determine to what the emotions are going to respond. The well-balanced man is the man who has struck a good balance between his intellect and his emotions. We find people giving vent to extreme emotional expression, who think that thereby they are being modern and up-to-date, but who, as a matter of fact, are merely chaotic. We misconstrue what Truth is because of our desire to express a thing as we want to do. There must be a conscious direction of that inner creative urge to express into channels which are happy, constructive, and in all ways profitable. We are not to "bottle" a desire to express, calling it evil or bad; we are to more greatly express and direct it in a constructive manner.

We are to view this great creative urge of Life as the eternal sun which shines beyond and through the mist and the cloud of uncertainty, that sun in whose beams we may bask at will. Every form of creation—the creative arts, the accomplishment of any purpose in life, the good that we do to each other, the kindly smile, the peaceful thought—is some part of that great Divine expression which balances and equalizes and makes sane our everyday life. When it comes to the art of spiritual mind treatment we shall find that it is this Creativity which is the Power that projects the word into form.

"Not every one that saith . . . Lord, Lord, shall enter into the kingdom of heaven. . . ." He who enters into a state of wholeness and completion is in a holy state. He who would know goodness, peace, and happiness must so enter into this native state of wholeness that he will find his prayer to be backed by conviction, his treatment filled with faith and feeling, and back of his whole outlook on life, perfect certainty. Such a man no longer walks the earth as downtrodden, disconsolate, and afraid. He knows that heaven is here, that God is his host, and he has further learned the great lesson which all people must learn, that he is today potentially a perfect and Divine being. We do not have to acquire Divinity; we have to reveal that Divinity which ever indwells us.

Love interprets Itself to everyone who knows love; comes to everyone who senses love; personifies Itself in forms which are human, in experiences which are Divine. We know that as we experience this indwelling Divinity, It becomes real. It is not an illusion; It is the great motivating Power of the universe. We touch It, revealed through this man, this woman, this child, and because they reflect that Love to us we "fall in love" with that person. It is God expressing through us. So we touch a Cause and we feel through that Cause a Divine and cosmic Reality.

As the unreality of the temporal is rolled away, the temporal does not pass from existence, it is translated into a new form; it comes as a Divine awakening. And looking at each other we see no longer the finite broken upon the wheel of circumstances, impoverished and sick, but we see back of the form that glorious Presence which tells us that gods are conversing with gods. The more universal a man becomes, the more sane he becomes, and the more he is able to appreciate the individual.

In learning to express Life, to give release to the Divine creative urge within us, we ultimately have to face the undeniable truth that thoughts do become things in our experience. What we need to do is to have our thoughts so conform to what we consider the nature of Spirit to be that nothing unlike Its inherent Good can become a part of our daily life.

The process of doing this through the practical use of Science of Mind is actually very simple. We train our minds to believe that there is a spiritual Presence within us which guides, controls, comforts, and heals. We put gently but firmly out of our minds those thoughts which deny this belief and persist in this belief until finally it becomes a part of our nature to believe that the Spirit through our minds responds to us and that we are daily re-created in the image of Perfection. We guard our thought against negative statement, against unbelief, until gradually we are living on the affirmative and constructive side of life.

There is no one living who cannot practice this simple method of spiritual healing. Do not refuse any good or comfort that can come on the physical plane. But realize this: There is That which transcends the physical, which is the builder, creator, sustainer, and arbiter of all that is. There is also that Thing in each one of us which is transcendent. As we learn to listen to this inner Presence, getting our impulse from It, we shall create our prayer, our spiritual mind treatment, after the perception received from It, and our increased awareness of Perfection will restore our body and affairs after a Divine pattern. So let each of us endeavor to heal himself and help to heal others of infirmities, troubles, and problems, not becoming discouraged, but always realizing that the possibility is here, that "there is a Divinity that shapes our ends,/ Rough-hew them how we will."

Your Great Experiment

O ne does not need to be unique to experience a higher degree of spirituality. However, there have been people, of all religious faiths, who have had spiritual perception, realization, or experience that has far transcended the ordinary experiences of daily living. These people, regardless of how crude or exalted their outward form of theology may have been, have at times so experienced God that God, to them, was real. This is what inner awareness is.

Those who have had such illuminating experiences of inner awareness have told us that they have been able to perceive that there was an absolute correspondence between the visible and invisible worlds. In other words, with the broader, deeper vision of spiritual perception they have been able to recognize that for every objective manifestation in the physical world there is what we may call today a subjective, or unseen, correspondent in the spiritual world. This would imply that what we actually see is but a reflection of an invisible image. This has been an experience common to all the great mystics who have so greatly influenced the course of religious thought.

The great spiritual geniuses of the ages have recognized that there is an invisible correspondent, or pattern, which is being reflected into what we term objective form. The objective form thus becomes not a thing in itself but exists as a reflection of a Cause which in Itself is intangible and is encompassed by neither time nor space. The tangible form is a reflection of Reality—the ultimate Cause and Source.

There does not appear to be anything in modern science or metaphysics that can, with any degree of validity, disagree with this viewpoint. In fact there is much today that confirms it.

The great problem of modern philosophy—and it was the problem of ancient philosophy—is the query as to how we get our images of thought. The great tendency of modern science is to reach out into the Invisible where there are adequate mental causes for this objective world which we call physical. Modern science supposes a certain hypothetical and theoretical Force of alleged motion and movement which no one knows anything about. This hypothetical and theoretical, but apparently mathematically conceived, operative Thing is what we call God or infinite Intelligence. Because we are intelligent, this infinite Intelligence must be the Source of our intelligence. The mind we use is the Mind of God functioning at the level of our conception of It. This is what Jesus meant when he said: "I can of mine own self do nothing . . . the Father that dwelleth in me, he doeth the works."

Now if there is a spiritual or a mental correspondent in the invisible world for every objective fact—from the greatest poem that was ever written, the greatest song that was ever sung, to the newest invention—then it naturally follows that not only must there be an invisible prototype or likeness of all that is which becomes visible according to Law, but also, if we can consciously create a prototype, according to the same Law that prototype will project itself into our environment. This is the practical angle of this very idealistic concept of the Universe.

Why, then, should not we be able to consciously create an image of thought and know that this same Law will cause it to be tangibly reflected in our environment? But, if the mind never gets beyond the place where it is controlled by its response to its physical environment or past memories, then the images it casts will be limited by these ideas.

Therein lies one of the apparent mysteries of the philosophy of Science of Mind, but one we can solve by experiment in our own lives.

For the most part we are hypnotized from the cradle to the grave. Why do we cry and laugh in the theater? Because we allow ourselves to be subject to the emotional reaction of what we witness. A person is a great actor, or a great orator, who is able to cause us to so react, but the influence is more or less hypnotic. In calmer moments we would say, "This is all a show; it is not going to affect me," and it would not.

If we could always let the intellect decide consciously what the emotions should respond to, we would save ourselves most of our emotional strain and, in all probability, many of our ailments would be practically eliminated because they seem to result from some form of tension or mental disturbance. We experience the physical correspondents of our patterns of thought, the prototypes we have created.

Nothing in this world can possibly happen by chance because the Universe is a thing of law and order. Hence, there must be a definite subjective cause for every physical effect. It does not matter whether a person is a materialist or idealist, this is a situation that does exist and sooner or later one will come to learn the practical aspects of it in daily living. Jesus said: "As thou hast believed, so be it done unto thee. . . ." And to make it more emphatic, in the story of the

Prodigal Son he taught what has been called the "reciprocal action" between the Universal and the particular. There is this Thing in the Universe which turns to us as we turn to It, through absolute correspondence.

Why, then, should we not consciously and definitely turn to It and provide for the action of the Law by mental images, spiritual realizations, or images of thought that shall no longer produce discord and disharmony? This is what spiritual mind treatment is. If a man turns to the creative Spirit within him, which does not foreordain limitation, lack, evil, or destruction, and creates in his thought through interior awareness, through spiritual perception, a mental equivalent of a better physical good, he is practicing the Science of Mind.

It is necessary in this world that we have the things that make us comfortable in this world. It is not only necessary, it is also right. But if we continue to maintain in our minds thoughts which are uncomfortable, it does not matter how good we are, they become the law of our lives. The Law of Mind is no respecter of persons. It does not say, "This man is good, I will honor him." The Law only knows us by reflection, by correspondence. It cannot know us any other way. So we bring what we call good or what we call evil upon us by the very Law of our being which is a Law of reflection.

Where are we going to get the ability to make our thoughts become the things we want, to create a happy situation, unless we can come to believe in spiritual equivalents? We shall never discover the Principle of Life by dissecting a corpse. We shall not find the spiritual Principle by dissecting any objective facts. Who by searching can find God? It is rather through that still, small voice, that inner perception, that interior awareness—"Be still, and know that I am God. . . ." If we wish to demonstrate a greater abundance it will not be done by continuing to think about lack. It is not easy to think happiness when we are unhappy, but we become the servant of our thoughts. As Tagore said: "The slave is busy making whips for his master." Our master is the Law of Cause and Effect. It serves us and then compels us to serve It as we have believed. It is at the same time heaven and hell; It is at once love and hate, freedom and bondage, because of Itself It is one Law, ready to take any form our thoughts establish for Its action.

Watch the life of a man who believes in God and the life of one who does not. The man who has a spiritual conviction lives in a different world from the one who does not have such a conviction. Unfortunately, too often our spiritual convictions come from theological dogmas and have a certain amount of sting in them, but even then they are better than none. There is no man on earth who is so forlorn as a materialist. There is nothing in the world so sad as unbelief.

How shall we find the equivalent of certainty? By so contemplating the eternal verities that doubt disappears. We shall find the equivalent for life and immortality by so dwelling on the idea that the Principle of Life cannot conceive death until the intellect perceives it and the mind accepts it. We go about seeking the fulfillment of joy, of peace, of certainty, and of security. This is what all the world wants, but we think these things are objective. They are not. Real as they are, they did not create themselves. They are but effects of a spiritual cause, which is an idea created by an act of the mind.

When all the world shall know that there is nothing to be afraid of, fear will disappear from the human mind forever, and not until then. But we cannot wait for that time. We must definitely and deliberately decide whether or not we are going to be afraid of anything. That is our decision; no one can make it for us. Nor is there any power in heaven or any belief in hell that can withhold the result of our decision from us.

We must right now develop this interior awareness, this spiritual perception which is a very real thing. If we embody the idea of confusion, we shall become confused, and if we maintain the idea of unhappiness, we shall become unhappy. But if we entertain the idea of peace long enough, we shall become peaceful. When we *know* freedom, freedom is ours.

It so happens in our lives that as we gradually discard and do away with discord, harmony then sits like a wreath of benediction on our brows. Can we, in the midst of the crowd, as Emerson said, keep "with perfect sweetness the independence of our solitude"? As we walk on the sidewalks of the city, can we stop seeing that which we no longer wish to experience and mentally embody only those ideas which we wish to experience? That is what practice is.

Spiritual mind treatment is for the purpose of consciously creating those states of mind which we should like to see tangibly manifested in the objective world. If we want to be prosperous, we must think nothing but success, no matter how much failure appears. If we want to gradually gravitate into the atmosphere of friendliness and love, we must know that the Universe is our friend, and if some person appears not to be friendly, we must utterly disregard it. We can convince the mind that our unity with Spirit is absolute, therefore we are *now* unifying with our good forevermore.

Our mind is an experimental laboratory. In it we can definitely prove for ourself, by specifically repudiating certain negative thoughts and dwelling on their opposites, that the eternal verities are real and ever present; that life is good, happy, complete, radiant, strong; that all the good there is is right here. Our mental equivalents, our spiritual concepts, our interior awarenesses are causative prototypes in the mind. They are not illusions, and our dynamic acceptance of them as realities causes the great universal Law to project a likeness of our acceptance on the screen of our experience.

DISCOVER THE WORLD
OF ERNEST HOLMES

The Landmark Guide to Spiritual Living

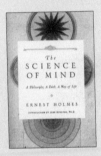

The Science of Mind: The Definitive Edition

A Philosophy, a Faith, a Way of Life

978-0-87477-865-6 (hardcover)

978-0-87477-921-9 (paperback)

The Science of Mind: The Complete Edition

Features the original 1926 and expanded 1938

editions—published together for the first time

978-1-58542-842-7 (paperback)

A Treasury of Inspiration and Guidance

A New Design for Living

978-1-58542-814-4

Love and Law

978-1-58542-302-6

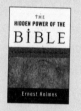

The Hidden Power of the Bible

978-1-58542-511-2

The Essential Ernest Holmes

978-1-58542-181-7

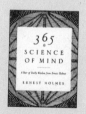

365 Science of Mind

978-1-58542-609-6

Prayer

978-1-58542-605-8

Simple Guides for Ideas in Action

Creative Mind 978-1-58542-606-5 · The Art of Life 978-1-58542-613-3

Creative Mind and Success 978-1-58542-608-9 · This Thing Called You 978-1-58542-607-2

Discover a Richer Life 978-1-58542-812-0 · Living Without Fear 978-1-58542-813-7

Think Your Troubles Away 978-1-58542-841-0 · It's Up to You 978-1-58542-840-3

Coming Soon

Questions and Answers on the Science of Mind

For more information:
www.penguin.com
TARCHER   www.tarcherbooks.com
PENGUIN   www.scienceofmind.com